Ancient Greece for Teens

An Enthralling Guide to Major Events and Figures in Greek History

© Copyright 2024 - All rights reserved.

The content contained within this book may not be reproduced, duplicated, or transmitted without direct written permission from the author or the publisher.

Under no circumstances will any blame or legal responsibility be held against the publisher, or author, for any damages, reparation, or monetary loss due to the information contained within this book, either directly or indirectly.

Legal Notice:

This book is copyright protected. It is only for personal use. You cannot amend, distribute, sell, use, quote, or paraphrase any part, or the content within this book, without the consent of the author or publisher.

Disclaimer Notice:

Please note the information contained within this document is for educational and entertainment purposes only. All effort has been executed to present accurate, up-to-date, reliable, and complete information. No warranties of any kind are declared or implied. Readers acknowledge that the author is not engaging in the rendering of legal, financial, medical, or professional advice. The content within this book has been derived from various sources. Please consult a licensed professional before attempting any techniques outlined in this book.

By reading this document, the reader agrees that under no circumstances is the author responsible for any losses, direct or indirect, that are incurred as a result of the use of the information contained within this document, including, but not limited to, errors, omissions, or inaccuracies.

Free limited time bonus

Stop for a moment. We have a free bonus set up for you. The problem is this: we forget 90% of everything that we read after 7 days. Crazy fact, right? Here's the solution: we've created a printable, 1-page pdf summary for this book that you're reading now. All you have to do to get your free pdf summary is to go to the following website: https://livetolearn.lpages.co/enthrallinghistory/

Or, Scan the QR code!

Once you do, it will be intuitive. Enjoy, and thank you!

Table of Contents

INTRODUCTION 1
CHAPTER 1: AN INTRODUCTION TO ANCIENT GREECE............................3
CHAPTER 2: GODS AND GODDESSES OF OLYMPUS.....................17
CHAPTER 3: THE RISE OF ATHENS FROM CITY-STATE TO EMPIRE......28
CHAPTER 4: BECOMING A SPARTAN 39
CHAPTER 5: THE PERSIAN WARS: MARATHON AND THERMOPYLAE 49
CHAPTER 6: THE GOLDEN AGE OF ATHENS: ART, PHILOSOPHY, AND DEMOCRACY 60
CHAPTER 7: THE PELOPONNESIAN WAR 71
CHAPTER 8: ALEXANDER THE GREAT...80
CHAPTER 9: THE HELLENISTIC AGE...90
CHAPTER 10: GREEK SCIENCE AND TECHNOLOGY.....................100
ANSWER KEY FOR ROUND-UP ACTIVITIES 109
HERE'S ANOTHER BOOK BY ENTHRALLING HISTORY THAT YOU MIGHT LIKE 117
FREE LIMITED TIME BONUS..118
BIBLIOGRAPHY 119
IMAGE SOURCES 122

Introduction

When you think of ancient Greece, what comes to mind? Great philosophers like Socrates and Plato? Majestic temples with stately pillars and marble statues? People wearing long, flowy garments? The birth of democracy? Ancient Greece was all that and so much more!

Ancient Greece was never a united country. Southern Greece did form an alliance to send the Persians packing, but it didn't create a central government. The Greeks briefly united under Alexander the Great, but Sparta wasn't on board. Ancient Greece was a group of powerful, independent city-states that loved to fight each other. When they weren't killing each other, the ancient Greeks did some pretty awesome things.

The Greeks wrote epic poetry, built colonies around the Mediterranean Sea, and invented the Olympic Games. Once every four years, they stopped fighting each other to run races in their birthday suits. Yes, clothing was optional. And let's not forget about philosophy! Some of it was a little crazy, but it was still impressive. The Greek pursuit of wisdom influenced how we think and do government today. They came up with the idea of democracy and forged ahead in science. Leucippus and Democritus figured out that constantly moving atoms form all matter. How could they know that?

The ancient Greek civilizations were famous for rising to astonishing heights until everything came crashing down. But they never stayed down. They would rise from the ashes, dust themselves off, and dash back into the fray, more brilliant than ever. When Xerxes marched on

Greece with his enormous army, the Greeks held the line. And we mean that literally. Six thousand Spartans held off the Persians for three days, sacrificing themselves to give southern Greece time to organize a defense.

The purpose of this book is to take you on an entertaining and enlightening journey through the history of ancient Greece. Don't ever think history is just a bunch of dry facts and dates to memorize. History is the story of people. Some were geniuses, and some were stupid beyond belief. Most were a little bit of both. On this journey, we'll learn what made the Greeks exceptional. This book will bring their stories to life with all their flaws and inconceivable victories.

What's the point of reading history? Some folks do it for fun; they find it fascinating. And it is, but that's not the only reason. When we understand the past, it helps us realize why things are the way they are today. For instance, why do most of today's governments have a senate and elected leaders? It all started in ancient Athens. History also teaches us the **catalysts for change.** What causes change? What speeds it up?

Let's travel back in time to unpack the astounding story of the ancient Greeks. Follow the jaw-dropping journey of their stunning inventions, discoveries, art, architecture, philosophy, religion, wars, and politics.

Chapter 1: An Introduction to Ancient Greece

This chapter will discuss Greece's spectacular physical features and walk the reader through a basic timeline. Next, it will explore ancient Greece's culture, focusing on the Archaic Age. Finally, it will unwrap ancient Greece's lasting legacy.

Geography

Greece is a land of enchanting beauty surrounded by sparkling seas. Steep, craggy hills and mountains cover 80 percent of Greece's mainland and islands. The mountains presented a problem. As Greece's population grew, it became harder to feed the people. The Greeks used **terraced farming**, carving a series of flat ledges on the hillsides to plant more crops. Yet, even with these terraces running up the hillsides, only one-fifth of the land could grow barley, grapevines, and olive trees.

Although the ancient Greeks grazed sheep and goats on the mountains and higher hills, the lack of land wasn't the farmers' only challenge. Greece gets almost no rain in the summer. Back then, agriculture depended on rainfall and snow in the winter, but that was unpredictable. Crop failure happened a lot. The farmers lost their grain crops about every four years. Deforestation and overgrazing made matters worse.

Beginning in the Archaic Age, Greece started sending some of its people away to feed those who remained. These colonists sailed to distant shores around the Mediterranean. They grew crops in fertile lands and then shipped grain back to Greece. So, it's fair to say that ancient Greece wasn't simply the land of modern Greece. It was an empire of colonies stretching from modern-day Spain to the west and Russia to the east.

Greece is surrounded by the Ionian Sea to the west, the Aegean to the east, and the Mediterranean to the south. The entire country

A vineyard growing on terraces on a steep hillside[1]

is one gigantic peninsula, and multiple smaller peninsulas stretch out like tentacles on an octopus. And then, there are the islands. Did you know that Greece has six thousand islands? Greece's early Cycladic people thrived on the islands in the Aegean Sea as fishermen and traders. They went spearfishing for tuna in primitive boats. Then, they began building ships with fifty rowers, which meant they could do deep-sea fishing. They could also sail to other lands. Greece became one of the world's premier sea traders.

Some of Greece's mountains are active volcanoes. Lava cooled to form obsidian, a black, razor-sharp glass. Obsidian was a hot trade item. Ancient people used obsidian for spears, arrowheads, knives, and other tools. Greece's islands were also rich in copper, iron, gold, silver, and marble. Greece exported minerals, wine, wool, olives, and exquisite ceramics.

Living near a volcano could be a nightmare. Around 1600 BCE, a volcano on the island of Thera erupted. It was disastrous. Ten million tons of rock and ash shot twenty miles (thirty-five kilometers) into the air.

Its VEI (volcanic explosivity index) was a seven. The highest VEI is an eight, but that has not happened in about twenty-seven thousand years. The Minoan eruption at Thera was like several atomic bombs exploding at once.

Fortunately, earthquakes and other signs must have warned the people living on Thera that something big was about to happen. Most folks must have sailed to safety before the eruption since few bodies were found. Two hundred feet (sixty meters) of pumice and ash buried anyone who didn't get away in time. The volcano caused a gigantic tsunami that flooded Crete's northern coast, almost 70 miles (110 kilometers) away. The tsunami washed away their splendid cities. Pumice even showered down on Egypt, which was 800 miles (1,287 kilometers) away.

Map of ancient Greece[2]

Timeline

Bronze Age (began about 3200 BCE in Greece)
- Minoans settled the island of Crete around 3500 BCE.
    - 2100 BCE: Minoans' great leap forward into a complex civilization
        - Constructed Europe's first cities and palaces
        - Built the world's first navy
        - Ruled the Aegean and Mediterranean Seas
        - Developed Europe's first writing system, Cretan hieroglyphics
    - 1800 BCE: Minoans developed Linear A writing with a phonetic alphabet
    - 1700 BCE: Earthquakes destroyed most cities in Crete, but they were rebuilt.
    - 1600 BCE: Minoan eruption on the island of Thera
    - Carved marble figurines of women with long necks and no lower legs
    - Buried their dead in tombs, which was advanced for this era in Greece
- Myceneans, a rising power around 1700 BCE
    - Thrived in southern Greece's Peloponnesian Peninsula and southern mainland
        - Seafaring traders and pirates
        - Built bridges, complex irrigation systems, and colossal walls.
    - 1420 BCE: Invaded Crete. Destroyed most cities but restored Knossos
    - Coexisted with Minoans on Crete until the Bronze Age collapse
    - 1400 BCE: Athens became a Mycenean city.
    - Adapted Linear B writing system from the Minoan's Linear A

- o 1200 BCE: The "mythical" Trojan War began when Myceneans attacked Troy in northwestern Turkey.
- Bronze Age Collapse (beginning 1200 BCE)
    - o Many cultures fell in Greece, the Middle East, and North Africa.
    - o Minoan, Cycladic, and Mycenean civilizations all collapsed.
    - o Most Greek cities fell except Athens; much of Greece's population died.
    - o Greece lost its writing system for three hundred years.
    - o Causes?
        - Environmental catastrophes, such as drought, volcanoes, and earthquakes
        - The "Sea Peoples," mysterious pirates who attacked coastal cities and crushed sea trade

The Dark Ages (1200–900 BCE)

Geometric Civilization (900–776 BCE)

- Produced ceramics with geometric designs
- The population grew, and cities were built again.
- Greeks began smelting iron in high-heat furnaces.
- 900 BCE: The Dorians rebuilt Sparta

Archaic Period (776–500 BCE)

- 776 BCE: The first Olympic Games launched the Archaic period
- 770 BCE: A fresh writing system began, loosely based on the Phoenician alphabet
    - o Over half the letters are in our alphabet today.
    - o Greeks began writing epic poetry.
        - Homer wrote the *Iliad* and the *Odyssey*.
        - Hesiod wrote *Theogony* and *Works and Days*.

- 750–550 BCE: Greek city-states established colonies around the Mediterranean, Aegean, Ionian, and Black Seas.
- 650 BCE: Sparta crushed the Messenian revolt.
- 621 BCE: Draco wrote the first written law code for Athens.
- 594 BCE: Solon wrote the first constitution for Athens.
- 580 BCE: The Punic Wars began; they continued on and off through the classical and Hellenistic ages.
- 550 BCE: Sparta established the Peloponnesian League with Corinth, Elis, and Tegea.
- 547 BCE: Wars with the Persian Empire began and continued for over a century.
- 508 BCE: Cleisthenes brought democratic reform to Athens.

Sprinters in the Olympics; notice the new Greek writing system above the runners.[3]

Classical Period (480–356 BCE)

- Golden Age of Athens (480–404 BCE)
- Greek coalition scored a great victory over the Persians.
    - o 480 BCE: Battle of Thermopylae – Spartans against a massive Persian army
    - o 479 BCE: Greek coalition trounced Persians in the naval Battle of Mycale.

- 477 BCE: Greek city-states formed the Delian League.
    - Kept the Persians out of the Aegean Sea for fifteen years
    - Rid seas of Dolopian pirates preying on Greek merchant ships
    - 460 BCE: Greece suffered a great loss when defending Egypt from Persia.
- 460–445 BCE: First Peloponnesian War between Sparta and Athens began.
- 451 BCE: Final face-off between Greece and Persia at Cyprus
    - Greeks crushed the Persian fleet.
    - Thirty-year Peace of Calais
- 431–404 BCE: Second Peloponnesian War
    - 430 BCE: Plague struck Athens, killing one-third of the population.
    - 404 BCE: Athens finally surrendered to Sparta.
- 399 BCE: Socrates was forced to commit suicide.
- 395-386 BCE: Corinthian Wars between Sparta and an alliance of Corinth, Thebes, Athens, Argos, and Boeotia
- 387 BCE: Persians formed King's Peace with Sparta, Athens, Argos, Corinth, and Thebes.
- 379 BCE: Thebes rose to power.
    - 375 BCE: Thebes defeated Sparta at the Battle of Tegyra.
    - 371 BCE: Battle of Leuctra: Thebes pulverized the Spartan forces.
    - Thebes invaded Thessaly and Macedon, taking young Prince Philip II hostage.

Macedonian-Greek Conquest of the Persian Empire (356–323 BCE)

- Philip II of Macedonia
    - 359 BCE: Became king of Macedonia
    - 358-340 BCE: Conquered Thrace and other lands north of Greece

- 352 BCE: Became ruler for life of Thessaly in northern Greece
- 338 BCE: Won Battle of Chaeronea and gained control of all Greece except Sparta
- 337 BCE: All Greek city-states (except Sparta) formed the League of Corinth.
    - Goal: A coordinated Macedonian-Greek conquest of the Persian Empire
    - An advance force of ten thousand men sent to Ionia (western coast of Turkey)
- 336 BCE: Philip was murdered by his ex-lover and bodyguard.

- Alexander the Great
    - 336 BCE: Became king of Macedonia, Thrace, and Greece after his father's death
    - 336-335: Reunited League of Corinth after Thrace, Athens, Thebes, and Thessaly pulled out
    - 334 BCE: Marched into Turkey with an army of forty thousand men
    - 334-333 BCE: Conquered western Turkey
    - 332 BCE: Took control of Lebanon, Syria, Judea, Gaza, and Egypt
    - 331 BCE: Fought Persian King Darius in Iraq and won
        - Darius fled; one of his governors then killed him.
        - Alexander then ruled the former Persian-Achaemenid Empire.
    - 330-324 BCE: Alexander conquered central Asia
        - Fell in love and married Roxana, daughter of a Bactrian chieftain
        - Explored Indian subcontinent
    - 323 BCE: Alexander became ill and died unexpectedly at age thirty-two.

The Hellenistic Age (323–27 BCE)

- 323-281 BCE: Wars of the Diadochi (Alexander's generals) were fought for control of the empire.
  - The empire was divided into several regions.
  - Seleucus, the last general, was killed in 281 BCE.
- The Hellenistic age blended Greek culture with Asian and Egyptian elements.
- 222 BCE: Sparta lost the Battle of Sellasia against Macedon; most male Spartans were killed.
- 215-205 BCE: First Macedonian War; Greek Aetolian League allied with Rome against Macedon
- 146 BCE: Rome conquered the Greek Achaean League at the Battle of Corinth.
  - Rome then dominated mainland Greece.
  - Greeks still ruled Egypt and western Turkey.
- 89-85 BCE: First Mithridatic War; Rome against Greek-controlled western Turkey
  - King Mithridates of Pontus (Turkey) took control of most of Greece.
  - 87 BCE: Rome's consul, Sulla, marched on Greece.
  - 86 BCE: Athens resisted but fell to Rome.

Culture

Greece's earliest known authors were Hesiod and Homer. They both wrote *epic poetry*, long poems that tell a story. The men and women in epic poems went on grand adventures. The stories usually involved the gods. Hesiod and Homer wrote at the very end of the Greek Dark Ages using Greece's new alphabet. Greece lost its earlier writing systems during the Dark Ages, which were mainly used for record-keeping, not literature.

Greek mythology says the hero Cadmus brought the Phoenician alphabet to Greece. The Greeks modified it for their own language, and it became the ancestor of the alphabet we use today.

Hesiod and Homer introduced literature to Greece. Their stories probably came from ancient tales retold by people for centuries. Homer wrote the *Iliad* and the *Odyssey* about the Trojan War and Odysseus's long journey home after the war.

Hesiod claimed to be a shepherd who met the nine Muses, goddesses of the arts, literature, and science. The Muses morphed Hesiod into a brilliant poet. In his poem, *Works and Days*, he told the story of creation, the great flood, and the five ages of man. The first age was the **Golden Age**, when the god Cronus created people. Everyone was good and got along with each other. No one knew pain or sadness. They ate fruit and vegetables and did not have to work hard.

A scene from a vase of three Muses playing a harp and lyres.'

It all fell apart when the god Zeus overthrew Cronus, which began the **Silver Age**. Now, folks had to work hard. They fought and quarreled with each other, but they still lived long lives, at least to the age of one hundred. Next came the **Bronze Age**, when people switched from being vegetarians to meat eaters. These warlike people were so corrupt, cruel, and violent that Zeus killed everyone in a flood.

Zeus kept one family alive, though. He noticed that Deucalion, his wife Pyrrha, and their son Hellen were honest and peaceful. Before opening the floodgates of heaven, Zeus told Deucalion to build an ark, fill it with food, and go inside. Then, the rain poured down, flooding everything and drowning all the violent people. Nine days later, the rain stopped. The ark rested on Mount Parnassus. Deucalion and his family came out on dry land and made a sacrifice to Zeus. Hellen's three sons formed the Achaean, Aeolian, and Dorian tribes, which repopulated Greece.

These three tribes began the next era, the Age of Heroes, when the Trojan War happened. The last age was the Iron Age, when Hesiod lived. He said the people of his age were brutal and self-absorbed. They were always tired and depressed. Hesiod warned that if folks didn't change, Zeus would also destroy this age.

During the "Age of Heroes," the city of Mycenae in southern Greece was the center of the Mycenaean civilization. Some of its massive twenty-foot-thick walls, built around 1250 BCE, still stand today. The stones in the walls were colossal. In later days, the Greeks looked at these boulders and decided that, even working together,

The Lion Gate at Mycenae was built almost 3,300 years ago.[5]

humans could not have possibly lifted them. "Only the Cyclopes could do this!" they exclaimed. The Cyclopes were mythical one-eyed, man-eating giants. Mycenae's gate has a twenty-ton lintel supported by two ten-foot boulders. It is called the Lion Gate after the carving of two lions over the lintel. Even today, people look at this structure and wonder how ancient humans got those stones up there.

As mentioned earlier, the Greeks established colonies around the Mediterranean, Aegean, Ionian, and Black Seas. These seas were the communication highways of the ancient world. How did this cultural mingling influence art and culture? People learned from each other by sharing ideas about painting, sculptures, pottery, and metalwork. The

Greek colonies opened schools that trained students to blend Greek ideas with Middle Eastern and Egyptian art. These schools taught things like making ceramics, carving ivory, cutting gems, and crafting jewelry and metalwork.

The Greek cities around the ancient world held competitions. Who could build the grandest and most elegant temples? **Lyric poetry** became popular in the Archaic age. These were short poems about emotions and romance sung to the playing of the *lyre* (something like a small harp). Greece's leading art centers were Corinth, Athens, and Sparta. The Corinthians painted silhouettes of plants and animals. Athenian vases had mythological scenes. The Spartans produced exquisite ivory carvings.

An amphora vase from Corinth with a silhouetted lion.[6]

Archaic Greece's philosophers made great leaps forward in many areas. Thales of Miletus, the "Father of Science," learned to predict solar eclipses. He explained a circle's diameter and the equal base angles of an isosceles triangle. The ancient Greeks believed that the god Atlas held the world on his shoulders. Thales's student Anaximander shocked everyone when he said the world was floating free in the universe. Anaximander's student, Anaximenes, taught that planets were not the same as stars. He figured this out by observing their movements over time.

Pythagoras said the earth wasn't flat but a sphere, like a ball. He developed the Pythagorean theorem for a ninety-degree triangle ($a^2 + b^2 = c^2$). Heraclitus of Ephesus talked about the *logos*. He said it was an invisible force that directed the universe. People must be in harmony with *logos* to understand reality.

Legacy

The Greek politician and commander Pericles said, "What you leave behind is not what is engraved in stone monuments, but what is woven into the lives of others." The legacy of the ancient Greeks is undoubtedly woven into our lives today. We owe an outstanding debt to them for their ideas and discoveries in art, architecture, philosophy, astronomy, medicine, and mathematics. When the Greeks exchanged ideas and knowledge around the Mediterranean and Asia, they birthed scholars who surged forward in science, math, and medicine. They took knowledge in many fields to new heights.

Greece influenced Roman religion, politics, philosophy, arts, and science. Today, this fusion of cultures is called the classical civilization or the Greco-Roman culture. This Greco-Roman culture impacted the Renaissance scholars and artists of western Europe. Greek artists portrayed the human form realistically in their sculptures, mosaics, and paintings, and the Renaissance artists copied this style. The majestic pillars that are the hallmarks of ancient Greek architecture still grace government buildings, churches, and mansions today. Ancient Athens and other Greek city-states pioneered democracy, which left its stamp on multiple nations today.

Round-up Activity: Timeline Game – What Happened When?

How well do you remember the order of key events in ancient Greece's history? Number these pivotal events in ancient Greece's history in the correct order.

( ) A catastrophic volcanic eruption wipes out all life on the island of Thera.

( ) A horrible plague kills one-third of Athens's population.

( ) Battle of Corinth: Rome conquers the Greek Achaean League.

( ) Cleisthenes brings democratic reform to Athens.

( ) First Olympic Games.

( ) The Greek Dark Ages.

( ) Minoans develop Greece's first writing system, Linear A.

( ) The Greek League of Corinth forms to invade the Persian Empire under Alexander.

( ) The Greeks unite to crush the Persian fleet in the naval Battle of Mycale.

( ) When Alexander the Great dies, his generals fight for control in the Wars of the Diadochi.

Check out the answer key at the end of the book, just before the bibliography. How well did you do?

Chapter 2: Gods and Goddesses of Olympus

Intrigue swirled around an unbelievably beautiful young woman named Helen. In the *Iliad* and the *Odyssey,* Homer said she was the daughter of the god Zeus and Queen Leda of Sparta. Greece's unmarried princes and kings gathered in Sparta bearing gifts. Each man hoped to make Helen his bride. Of course, Helen had no say in the matter. It was up to the man she called father: Tyndareus, Leda's husband and Sparta's king.

Sweat dripped from King Tyndareus's brow. Who should he choose? No matter what man he picked, everyone else would be angry. What if they attacked Sparta?

Odysseus, the cunning prince of Ithaca, came to the rescue. He was one of the few men in Greece not interested in marrying Helen. He was madly in love with Penelope, the daughter of Sparta's other king, Icarius. Yes, Sparta had two kings; we'll get into that later. Odysseus told Tyndareus he would help him with his Helen problem if he would put a good word in for Odysseus with Icarius. The two men agreed, and Odysseus gave his advice.

"All the men who want to marry Helen must swear a sacred oath. They must vow to defend Helen's marriage to whomever you choose. They must swear that no matter what, they will not attack you or the man you select as her husband. Furthermore, if anyone steals Helen from the husband you choose, all the others must vow to bring her back."

"Was this the face that launched a thousand ships? Sweet Helen, make me immortal with a kiss!"
– Christopher Marlowe.[7]

Tyndareus had everyone swear the oath, and they sacrificed a horse to seal the deal. Tyndareus chose Menelaus, prince of Mycenae, as Helen's husband. Helen had secretly hoped he'd pick Menelaus, so she breathed a sigh of relief. Menelaus and Helen married. They had several children and lived happily together for ten years. Tyndareus convinced his co-king, Icarius, to give his daughter Penelope in marriage to Odysseus. Everything was rosy for the two young couples until the goddess Aphrodite interfered.

It all started with a beauty contest for the prize of a golden apple. The goddesses Hera, Athena, and Aphrodite asked Zeus to decide which of them was the most beautiful. Zeus wasn't about to get involved in that messy affair, so he asked Paris to judge the contest. Paris was the prince of Troy, which was located in northwestern Turkey. He jumped at the chance. Three gorgeous goddesses—what could possibly go wrong?

Each of the goddesses offered a bribe to Paris. Hera said he could rule Europe and Asia if he chose her. Athena bribed him with superhuman warrior skills. Aphrodite promised him the love of Helen, the world's most beautiful woman. She forgot to tell him that Helen was already married, though. Paris chose Aphrodite as the most beautiful goddess, and she helped him steal Helen from Menelaus. Was Helen kidnapped, or did she go willingly? No one is quite sure. But Menelaus was hellbent on getting his wife back, and that was how the Trojan War began.

The Greeks were *polytheistic*, which means they worshiped many gods. However, their gods were like ordinary humans but with superpowers. They cheated on their spouses, lied, stole, quarreled, and tricked humans. They might intervene to help the humans they liked, but they could just as easily make someone's life miserable. Their erratic and selfish behavior irritated the Greek philosopher Socrates. "How can we expect people to be good if the gods aren't?" he ranted.

Who Were the Twelve Olympians?

The highest mountain in Greece is Mount Olympus. The ancient Greeks thought it was the home of the most important gods, the Twelve Olympians. They were Zeus, Hera, Aphrodite, Apollo, Ares, Artemis, Athena, Demeter, Hephaistos, Hermes, Poseidon, and Dionysus. Some lists have Hestia, the goddess of the hearth, instead of Dionysus. What were the roles and attributes of these twelve gods?

Zeus (or maybe Poseidon).[8]

Zeus was the king of the gods. He was the storm god, which was incredibly important in a land desperate for rainfall. He was responsible for ensuring that the gods and humans lived orderly lives. That didn't always pan out, especially since Zeus wasn't particularly orderly himself. Maybe it stemmed from his childhood trauma. His father, Cronus, ate his brothers and sisters. Zeus survived because his mother, Rhea, hid him on the island of Crete.

When Zeus grew up, he confronted his father and made him vomit up his siblings. He married his sister **Hera**, but that proved problematic. Hera was insanely jealous because Zeus would shapeshift into other forms to seduce women who were unaware of his true identity.

Hera, queen of the gods, took her wrath out on her husband's lovers and their children. For instance, she turned Callisto into a bear. Heracles (Hercules in Roman myths) was an illegitimate son of Zeus. Hera sent snakes to kill him when he was a baby. When that failed, and he grew up, she made Heracles insane. He killed his wife and children. In the Trojan War, Hera supported the Greeks because Prince Paris of Troy chose Aphrodite over her in the beauty contest.

Hera forced **Aphrodite**, the goddess of love and war, to marry her son, **Hephaistos** (known as Hephaestus in Roman mythology). He was the disabled god of crafts and volcanos. Hera abandoned him at birth, but he still became one of the Twelve Olympians. Aphrodite was unfaithful. Homer wrote that Hephaistos divorced her and demanded back the bride price he had paid at the wedding.

Red-on-black pottery with Dionysus walking and Hephaistos riding a donkey.[9]

20

Aphrodite mischievously used her powers to make the gods fall in love with human females. But her magic came back to haunt her when she saw a Trojan prince, Anchises, playing his lyre while tending his cattle. She draped herself in golden robes and revealed herself to Anchises, who fell under her spell. Aphrodite gave birth to Aeneas, who was raised as a prince in Troy. She guarded him through the Trojan War, saving him from being killed several times. After Troy fell, Aeneas traveled to Italy, and his descendants founded Rome.

Everyone loved **Apollo**, the god of the sun, music, archery, and healing. Well, maybe the Greeks didn't love him so much during the Trojan War since he supported Troy. Apollo saved the lives of Aeneas and his cousin Hector several times. He struck the Greeks with the plague and sent Paris's arrow into Achilles's heel, killing the great warrior. But after the war, the Greeks resumed their adoring worship of this handsome young god. He frequently appeared on Greek coins.

Ares was the unpopular god of war. He would get angry over trivial things and was always looking for a fight. Ares and Aphrodite had a fling, but Aphrodite's husband, Hephaistos, found out. Hephaistos designed a golden net that wrapped around the couple when they were in bed. He called the rest of the gods to witness the couple's infidelity. The gods encircled the bed, roaring with laughter at the embarrassed twosome. Hephaistos finally released them, and they slunk off in shame.

Artemis was the goddess of nature, wild animals, and hunting. Although she was a virgin, she was the deity of fertility and childbirth. When she was a little girl, her father Zeus asked what he could give her as a gift. She asked for all the mountains in the world because that was where she wanted to spend her time. Artemis healed Aphrodite's son, Aeneas, when he was wounded in the Trojan War. When Agamemnon, King of Mycenae, killed a deer in her sacred grove, she demanded the sacrifice of his daughter. If he refused, Artemis would stop the wind, and he wouldn't be able to sail to Troy. Agamemnon prepared to sacrifice the girl, but Artemis took pity at the last minute and made her a priestess in her temple.

Artemis is in the Bible. The apostle Paul was traveling through the Greek colonies on the western coast of Turkey. He stayed in Ephesus for two years, discussing the Christian faith in the city's lecture hall every day. Extraordinary miracles occurred through Paul in Ephesus, where Artemis was the patron goddess. The silversmiths got riled up because no one was buying statues of Artemis anymore. "He says that man-made gods are no gods at all!" The silversmiths led a protest, where a crowd shouted for two hours, "Great is Artemis of the Ephesians!"

Athena was the goddess of war, wisdom, and crafts. She was intelligent, brave, and a brilliant problem solver. Athena was the patron goddess of Athens, her namesake. Like Artemis, she was a virgin who didn't get involved in messy affairs. Hesiod said that Zeus swallowed his first wife, Metis, while

Athena.[10]

she was pregnant. He was terrified that she would give birth to a son who would overthrow him, just as he had done to his father, Cronus. Athena burst through her father's head as a grown woman wearing armor. Despite splitting her father's skull open, she was Zeus's favorite child.

Athena helped the Greeks break into Troy by giving Odysseus the idea of using the Trojan Horse. Thirty-two Greek warriors hid inside an enormous wooden horse while the rest of the Greeks sailed away. They didn't go too far, though. The Trojans thought the Greeks had abandoned the war and brought the horse inside. That night, the warriors inside the horse crept out and opened the city gates for the other Greeks.

Demeter was Zeus's sister. She was an earth goddess who helped farmers and ensured the earth's fertility. She had two children with Zeus:

Persephone and Iacchus. She got involved with a mortal man named Iasion, and Zeus killed him with a thunderbolt.

Hades, the god of the underworld, fell in love with Demeter's daughter Persephone and kidnapped her. Zeus wasn't interested in rescuing his daughter, so Demeter cursed the land, causing the rain to stop and all crops to die. Zeus finally commanded Hades to release Persephone. While she was in the underworld, she had eaten a pomegranate seed, so she had to return to the underworld for several months each year.

Hermes was the creative and playful god of wealth, livestock, gamblers, thieves, and travel. With his winged sandals, he could travel quickly between the world of humans and the world of gods. He served as the gods' messenger. Hermes also guided souls to the River Styx in their journey to the underworld. He introduced the alphabet, fire, panpipes, the lyre, and dice to humans. He was always up to mischief. He stole Apollo's cattle, but Apollo let him keep them in exchange for Hermes's lyre. Hermes supported the Greeks in the Trojan War and assisted Odysseus on his long journey home by helping him escape the sorceress Circe.

Poseidon was the god of rivers, seas, floods, earthquakes, and horses. Although he often brought destruction, he was seen as the protector of sailors. Poseidon lived under the ocean in a golden mansion. He was the father of the one-eyed Cyclopes, the winged horse Pegasus, and Charybdis, the sea monster that created whirlpools to sink ships so she could eat them.

Poseidon had a crush on Princess Scylla. His jealous wife, Amphitrite, turned her into a monster with six snake heads. Scylla ate sailors, including six of Odysseus's friends.

Dionysus was the god of wine, insanity, theater, and festivals. Dancers at festivals dedicated to Dionysus got into such a frenzy that they entered an altered state. King Midas of Phrygia rescued Dionysus's friend, so the god granted him a wish. Midas wished that everything he touched would be turned to gold. That became problematic when he couldn't eat because his food turned to gold. Worst yet, when he hugged his daughter, the little girl turned to gold. To his relief, Dionysus reversed the wish.

How Did the Ancient Greeks Worship Their Gods?

The ancient Greeks honored their gods by pouring out wine. They also sacrificed animals, such as bulls, sheep, goats, pigs, and geese. They sacrificed animals in the courtyard of a temple. The priests examined the animals' intestines to see into the future. They burned some of the bones and fat on the altar, and everyone ate the rest of the meat.

Ancient Greeks gave **votive offerings** to thank the gods for answering a prayer. They also made votive offerings when making a vow. A votive offering could be any number of things, including small images of the god, figurines of people praying, weapons, vases, or jewelry. The temples became storehouses for a vast number of votive offerings. Greek temples were usually within a walled sanctuary with gardens, fountains, statues, sacred trees, and altars.

The Oracle of Delphi advising a visiting king.[11]

Both men and women served as priests. Generally, goddesses had priestesses, and the male deities had male priests. Certain places, like Delphi, had a female *oracle*. The Oracle of Delphi was a priestess called Pythia. She would sit on a stool straddling a crevice from which fumes wafted up. Greek myth said the fumes were from the rotting body of the Python monster killed by Apollo. As she breathed in the fumes of the decaying dragon, she entered into a trance and could then answer the questions of those seeking advice.

Festivals were an essential part of the ancient Greek religion. The Olympic Games were one of these festivals. After sacrificing a hundred bulls to Zeus, everyone sat down to enjoy a grand barbeque. Only men could compete in the games. Married women could not attend. Maybe their husbands didn't want them to see the other naked men in the races. Single girls could attend. They had their own athletic competitions to honor Hera. The young women athletes wore short tunics with their hair loosely flowing down their backs.

Who Won the Trojan War? Did It Really Happen?

King Menelaus of Sparta wanted to get his wife back from Prince Paris of Troy. He reminded the other Greek kings of the oath they had sworn to defend his marriage. However, the other kings were hesitant. Troy was a powerful walled city guarded by fierce warriors. All the Greek city-states would need to send ships and soldiers if they had any hope of winning. They knew the war would come at great cost. And yet, taking control of Troy meant controlling the Dardanelles, a narrow strait in western Turkey that ran from the Aegean Sea to the Sea of Marmara. From there, ships could sail into the Black Sea. Controlling the Dardanelles meant gaining unimaginable wealth from trade.

For many years, most people considered the Trojan War a myth. Yet, the ancient Greek historians spoke of it as a historical fact, describing the city of Troy in detail and dating the war to around 1200 BCE. Recent evidence suggests the war really did happen. Homer said another name for Troy was Wilusa. The Hittites lived in western Turkey. Their records named Wilusa as a city in their empire. The Hittite chronicles speak of a prince named Alaksandu, which Homer said was another name for Paris.

In 1870, an amateur archaeologist named Heinrich Schliemann teamed up with Charles Maclaren and Frank Calvert to explore an archaeological site called Hissarlik at the southern end of the Dardanelles. Civilizations would build on top of the same site, and this site had nine layers of civilization. One layer had a dome and other architecture that matched Homer's description of Troy. This layer was suddenly destroyed around 1180 BCE, about the same time the Greeks said that Troy fell. Most scholars agree this city was ancient Troy.

Homer's *Iliad* says that King Agamemnon of Mycenae led an alliance of the Greek city-states against Troy. Agamemnon was the brother of Menelaus, who wanted Helen back. The Greeks sailed one thousand ships to Troy and fought for ten years. The Greek forces finally got inside the walls. They killed most of the Trojan warriors and burned down the city. Probably the only winner was King Menelaus, who got Helen back. But he and everyone else lost many dear friends in the fierce fighting. The Greeks crushed Troy, but it was a bitter victory. After being away for a decade, they returned home to find their wives with other men and their cities in chaos.

Menelaus and his dead friend Patroclus.[12]

Round-up Activity: Who's Who?

Match each of the Twelve Olympians with their description. Check your answers using the answer key at the back of the book.

1. Aphrodite   A. King of the gods and of rain

2. Apollo   B. Queen of the gods and vengeful wife of Zeus

3. Ares   C. Goddess of love and mother of Aeneas

4. Artemis   D. The disabled god of crafts and volcanoes

5. Athena   E. God of the sun, music, archery, and healing

6. Demeter   F. God of war and one of Aphrodite's lovers

7. Dionysus   G. Goddess of nature, wild animals, and hunting

8. Hephaistos   H. Goddess of wisdom who split open Zeus's head

9. Hera   I. Goddess of farmers and the earth's fertility

10. Hermes   J. The messenger god with winged sandals

11. Poseidon   K. God of the seas and father of the Cyclopes

12. Zeus   L. God of wine, insanity, theater, and festivals

Chapter 3: The Rise of Athens from City-State to Empire

The thriving Mycenaean civilization was a distant memory. The few surviving people lived in small villages, where they farmed, herded animals, and fished. Greece lingered in its Dark Ages for three centuries, from around 1200 to 900 BCE. Because the Greeks lost their writing system, it's hard to know what happened.

The Bronze Age Collapse

It wasn't only Greece that crashed during the Bronze Age collapse. Several other civilizations in western Asia suddenly fell. Why did people abandon these cities? What caused so many people to die? Although the Greeks did not leave a written record, the Egyptians and Syrians did. Additionally, archaeologists can explore the ruins of ancient cities for clues like earthquake damage or destruction by an invader.

Scientists can also study core samples from lake, river, and sea bottoms. Low pollen counts mean a lack of rainfall killed off plants. Stalagmites in caves are formed by water seeping down. Scientists can analyze stalagmites for their mineral content, which tells them about oxygen and carbon levels. Tree rings show how much rain fell each year and what the temperatures were.

The Bronze Age collapse was the perfect storm of environmental disasters and invasions. A deadly drought struck the area that is Israel and Palestine today. Greece suffered an "earthquake storm" from 1225 to 1175 BCE along a weakened fault line. The earthquakes toppled cities and caused tsunamis that flooded coastal areas. King Musili II of the Hittites wrote of a terrible plague that caused many people to get sick and die for over twenty years.

Remember, this was at the very end of the Trojan War. The ten-year war had emptied the treasuries of the Greek cities and killed many of its young men. There weren't enough husbands for the young women. Greeks usually didn't practice *polygamy* (marriage to more than one person). Fewer married couples meant fewer children and smaller populations. Some kings returned to find someone challenging their right to rule. Leadership struggles probably toppled some cities.

Lastly, the mysterious Sea Peoples invaded Greece, Egypt, Syria, and the Hittite Empire. They were savage pirates who raided cities around the eastern Mediterranean Sea. They stole food and burned cities down. Since they ruled the seas, they broke down the sea trade on which Greece and other civilizations depended.

One Egyptian pharaoh wrote that the Sea Peoples came from the "northern seas." The Egyptians said they traveled south in wagons with their families and possessions. Could these Sea Peoples be survivors from Troy looking for a place to resettle? Another theory is that once Troy fell, no one was there to guard the link from the Black Sea to the Mediterranean Sea. The Sea Peoples could have come from what is today's Ukraine or Russia. They might have been displaced by some catastrophe, such as climate change from a volcanic eruption.

Rising from the Ashes

Around 900 BCE, Greece began crawling out of its slump. Trade picked up, and the population doubled quickly. Restored ancient cities rose into cultural centers. The Greeks developed smelting technology, which allowed them to make iron weapons and tools. In 776 BCE, Greece celebrated its first Olympic Games, beginning the *Archaic period* (776-500 BCE). The Greeks started writing again with a new alphabet. Greece shone brighter than ever before.

Athens was the only major city in Greece that survived the Dark Ages. Once the threat from the Sea Peoples faded, Athens became the chief trade hub in Greece. It took control of the entire Attica Peninsula, ruling its towns and cities in a mini-empire. As Athens grew wealthy, it helped bring wealth to the rest of Greece.

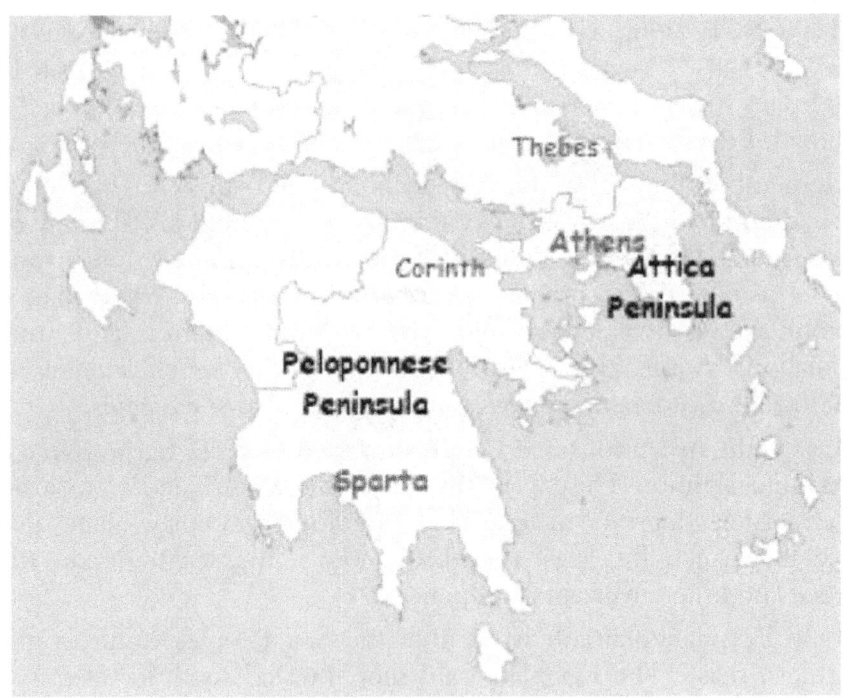

Ancient southern Greece.[13]

City-states

In Greece's Archaic era, various regions formed *city-states*. A city-state was a sizeable ruling city that controlled the smaller cities, towns, villages, and farmland surrounding it. It was like a small country.

Ancient Greece had no central government. Each city-state was independent. An interesting aspect was that each city-state did its own thing. Some had kings, some had a council of ruling elders, some had tyrants, and some began experimenting with democracy. Many of the city-states cycled through several types of government. As Greece rebounded, it grew to include over one thousand city-states. Athens, Sparta, and Corinth were the leading three city-states.

An Empire of Colonies: "Frogs around a Pond"

The city-states sent out expeditions to colonize new territories. They settled in northern Greece, Turkey's islands, and southern Italy. So many Greeks lived in southern Italy that it was nicknamed *Magna Graecia* (Great Greece). There were many colonies spread around the

Mediterranean, stretching as far as Spain and France. The Greeks sailed to the Black Sea and founded colonies around its shores. Plato said they were "like frogs around a pond."

Most of the colonies were independent of the city-state that sent the expeditions there. However, they had great loyalty to their mother city. If the main city-state fell under attack, they would send troops to defend it. By the end of the Archaic era, about 40 percent of the Greek population lived in colonies outside of Greece. There were around five hundred colonies. They sent athletes back to Greece every four years to compete in the Olympic Games.

Unlike other city-states, Athens continued to control its colonies, making it a true empire. Athens had governmental centers for the colonies in a particular area. For instance, the island of Samos in the eastern Aegean Sea had a council that made laws and collected taxes from the nearby colonies. The colonists from Athens kept their citizenship, which did not happen with other city-states. The Athenian colonies had their own militaries, but the officers came from Athens. The colonies could not go to war on their own. Athens first colonized the islands and coastline of the Aegean Sea. Later, it spread its colonial empire to the Black Sea, southern Italy, and Sicily.

The Rocky Path to Democracy

Athens had kings in the Mycenean era and the Dark Ages. The kings led a council of nobles who owned land. In the early Archaic period, Athens had three *archontes* (rulers). One was in charge of the government, one oversaw the military, and one led religion. An assembly of aristocratic male citizens (the *Ecclesia*) elected these three men from the nobility.

An attempted overthrow rocked Athens in 632 BCE. An Olympic athlete named Cylon tried to grab power. Cylon wanted to become Athens's tyrant, but he wasn't sure how to do it. So, he visited the Oracle of Delphi and asked her advice. The Oracle was sometimes cryptic in what she told people. The Oracle told Cylon to take power in Athens during a feast for Zeus. Cylon mulled this over. A feast for Zeus? Did she mean the Olympic Games?

Temple of Athena Nike in Athens.¹⁴

Cylon must have gotten the wrong festival because his attempt to take Athens did not go well. The Athenians fought hard to defend their city. Cylon escaped, but his soldiers hid out in the Temple of Athena. The temple was sacred ground, and the Athenians could not touch the men as long as they were in the temple. The soldiers had nothing to eat or drink. After a few days, they were desperate.

The Athenians promised Cylon's troops they wouldn't kill them if they surrendered. So, they laid down their weapons and came out. However, the Athenians broke their word and stoned them to death. By doing this, Athens's leaders broke the sacred "law of suppliants" (a *suppliant* is someone seeking mercy or forgiveness). Athens's leaders had to go into exile, and a curse followed them because they defiled Athena's temple.

The Athenians decided that part of the problem was that they didn't have any written laws. The rich rulers were constantly changing the laws to suit their needs. Sometimes, they pretended a particular law didn't exist. If they had written laws, it would clear matters up. So, in 621 BCE, they approached a nobleman named Draco and asked him to write down the laws. Draco didn't make up new laws for Athens. He just wrote down the unwritten laws that everyone was supposed to follow.

Draco's punishments for breaking laws were harsh. He ordered the death penalty for almost everything, even for something as trivial as stealing a cabbage. People who couldn't pay their debts became slaves. His harsh laws gave us the word ***draconian***, which means something inhumane or unusually cruel.

On a positive note, Draco gave all Athenians equal legal rights. It didn't matter if they were aristocrats or commoners, wealthy or poor. The same laws applied to everyone. Previously, only wealthy landowners could vote or hold political positions. Now, military men could vote and serve in minor political positions. Draco paved the way for democracy to take root in Athens.

Nevertheless, the Athenians worried about the death penalty. In 594 BCE, they approached Solon, a poet and philosopher, and asked him to write a constitution. Solon got rid of Draco's law code. In Solon's opinion, the unrest in Athens was caused by the oppression of the poor and middle classes.

Solon started by "shaking off" the crushing debt that kept people down. The aristocrats had been seizing land from farmers if a lousy harvest kept them from paying their debt. Some people put themselves or their children up as security when taking out a loan. If they couldn't pay in time, they or their children became slaves. Solon

Solon.[15]

canceled all debts. He freed those who had been enslaved because they were behind on their payments.

Solon's constitution divided the Athenians into four classes. Most people were in the lower class, and some got to vote for the first time. The four classes each sent one hundred men to the four-hundred-man council. All levels of society had equal representation. The city now had a balance of power. Back then, though, only the men were represented. Women couldn't vote in Greece until 1952 CE. It still wasn't a true democracy because even most men couldn't vote. Yet, it was a giant step in the right direction.

Solon made other reforms. He felt that marriages should be based on love, not on the money or property a man could get from his bride's *dowry* (gifts that were given to a spouse). Solon banned dowries. He also banned gossip and hate speech. Solon improved the court system by allowing poor people to have someone to defend them. Many of the judges were corrupt. Now, people could appeal to the four-hundred-man council if they didn't like a judge's ruling.

The lower classes loved Solon's constitution because it gave them more rights. But Solon knew it created enemies among the rich and powerful. He skipped town as soon as he finished the constitution and didn't return for ten years. When he came back, he was horrified to see Athens in **anarchy** (lawlessness and disorder because of the government's breakdown). The council had not elected an **archon** (political leader) in two years.

Tyrant Takeover

What's worse, Solon's cousin Peisistratus made himself a tyrant of Athens. What is a tyrant? When we hear that word today, we think of a power-hungry, oppressive ruler. Back then, a tyrant wasn't the enemy of freedom. A tyrant came into power outside of the usual way. A tyrant wasn't a hereditary king. A council didn't select him, and he wasn't elected. Tyrants were **usurpers** who grabbed political power by force.

A tyrant was not necessarily evil. Yes, he had absolute power. He did not necessarily follow the laws of a city-state. But tyrants could improve the lives of ordinary people. A tyrant kept his position by keeping the people happy. Tyrants did things like build roads, bridges, and water systems. They created jobs for farmers and soldiers who had lost their land.

Peisistratus developed an army out of the lower classes. Solon might have doubted his cunning cousin, but Peisistratus proved to be a fair and generous ruler. His family had silver and gold mines in Macedonia, and he used his income to buy back the farmers' land. He repaired and enhanced Athens's *infrastructure* (public works like roads, sewers, and bridges). He taught the farmers how to make a profit by exporting wine and olive oil.

Peisistratus ruled Athens for five years until his enemies became powerful enough to banish him. A man named Megakles said he would help Peisistratus get back into power if he married his daughter. Megakles dreamed of having a grandson who ruled Athens. The two men agreed to the deal, but they faced a challenge. How would they get the Athenians on board, especially the rich and powerful?

They found a tall, beautiful young woman to help them with their plan. She dressed like the goddess Athena and rode in a fine chariot into Athens. "Peisistratus is the greatest of men! I want him to rule Athens!" The Athenians thought she really was the goddess and obeyed her. Peisistratus was in power again but only for a brief time. He married Megakles's daughter but refused to sleep with her. He didn't want her to have sons that would challenge his sons from his first marriage.

Peisistratus and the fake Athena.[16]

An angry Megakles drove Peisistratus out of Athens again. Peisistratus languished in exile for ten years. He used the money from his mines in Macedonia to hire *mercenaries* (soldiers who fought for another city-state or country for money). He allied with several other Greek city-states and retook Athens in 546 BCE. This time, he ruled for almost two decades until he died.

During his third reign, Peisistratus launched significant reforms. He taxed the rich landowners 10 percent of their income. This money funded loans for poor farmers. He transformed the farming system in the Attica Peninsula, making it highly productive. Athens dominated trade around the Mediterranean and Black Seas. Peisistratus rebuilt Athena's temple and developed Athens into a destination for festivals and theater.

Groundbreaking Democratic Reforms

After Peisistratus died, Athens descended into disorder again. The Spartans overthrew Athens, but the Athenians were able to get rid of them. They made Megakles's son, Cleisthenes, their new leader.

Cleisthenes wasted no time turning Athens's politics around. He reorganized the entire Attica Peninsula into ten tribes, each of which included people from the three different geographical regions around Athens, ensuring a more balanced distribution of political power. The tribes had representatives from the city of Athens, the coastal towns, and the farm villages. Each tribe sent fifty men to serve on the council for one year. Only the five hundred men on the council could vote, but they represented all levels of society. This early form of democracy continued into Greece's classical period.

Round-up Activity: Word Search

There are ten key words/phrases hidden in the puzzle. Read the definitions below to figure out the key word, then find it in the puzzle. The answer key is at the back of the book.

E	S	P	A	L	L	O	C	E	G	A	E	Z	N	O	R	B
T	I	N	I	N	F	R	A	S	T	R	U	C	T	U	R	E
A	E	M	C	A	W	X	A	N	Y	M	A	G	Y	L	O	P
T	R	L	E	I	V	Y	E	L	A	R	O	U	D	S	W	L
S	A	K	A	N	U	A	R	L	G	R	F	N	R	Y	O	L
Y	N	J	R	O	T	Z	S	Y	A	E	C	D	O	E	T	I
T	E	I	G	C	S	H	R	C	U	E	U	H	W	T	R	T
I	C	H	A	A	R	W	I	O	T	N	A	R	Y	T	D	S
C	R	G	N	R	O	I	Y	O	O	H	O	A	E	W	S	U
D	E	R	G	D	Q	S	R	L	Y	A	Y	L	H	H	A	O
C	M	E	A	O	P	T	O	D	O	V	E	L	T	A	R	Y
B	A	Y	M	W	T	S	R	N	L	G	D	U	M	I	E	A

1. The sudden fall of multiple civilizations in the eastern Mediterranean around 1200 BCE
2. Marriage to more than one person
3. One large independent city ruling over towns and villages in the surrounding area
4. "Great Greece" region of southern Italy
5. An absolute ruler who comes to power outside the usual channels

6. Something inhumane or unusually cruel
7. Money or property a bride brings into a marriage
8. Disorder because of governmental breakdown
9. Public works like roads, bridges, and sewers
10. Soldiers who are paid to fight for another city-state or country

Chapter 4: Becoming a Spartan

The Spartans always marched to a different drum. When everyone else in Greece was doing one thing, they took an alternative path. For instance, Athens was progressive in its politics, and its citizens were always eager to discuss the latest ideas. The Spartans weren't big fans of change. They liked to keep things the way they were. Philosophy was for weaker people. They focused on building muscular bodies and iron wills.

Everything in Sparta revolved around the military. Fighting was a sacred job. Warriors were glorified as the core of Spartan society. Children did not belong to their parents but to the state. Every boy was considered a future soldier. Parents brought their newborn babies to the council, called the Gerousia, to evaluate their health and strength. If a baby didn't pass the inspection, it would be placed on a mountain to die.

Peculiar Politics

While other cities experimented with democracy and tyrants, Sparta stuck with its system of two kings. Why two kings? Well, Sparta started out with one king, whom they believed was descended from the hero Heracles. In Sparta's early days, lightning struck and killed King Aristodemus. He left identical twin baby sons. Which one should be king? The babies looked so much alike that no one could tell them apart. Even their mother claimed she couldn't be sure which was born first. The elders traveled to Delphi to ask the Oracle what to do. She said to make both of them kings, and that's what they did.

From that point on, Sparta kept the two-king system. This came in handy when Sparta was at war. One king could lead the army as commander in chief, while the other stayed in Sparta and kept things running smoothly. The system also provided a system of **checks and balances.** Neither king held complete power. Each contributed his own ideas, so the rule was more balanced. If one king's action plan was not a good move, the other king could "check" or block it.

Sparta had a ruling council, as most of Greece's cities did, but everyone on Sparta's council was at least sixty years old. All the younger men were off fighting battles. Sparta's council of twenty-eight elderly men was an *oligarchy* (a small group of people running political affairs). The two kings served on the council as the only ones under sixty. The kings took turns leading the troops in battles and serving as priests and judges.

Schooling Sparta's Soldiers

All Spartan men served full time in the military beginning at age twenty. They retired at age sixty. At the tender age of seven, Spartan boys left home to join the *agoge* training system, where they lived in dormitories with other boys. In the agoge, they trained in military skills, hunting, reading, writing, singing, and dancing. The boys learned to tolerate pain and live simple "Spartan" lives with plain food and no frills.

The Spartan training had three levels. From age seven to twelve, the boys trained in the first level, the *paides.* They then joined the *paidiskoi* for the rest of their teen years. Initiation into the paidiskoi was harsh, but it prepared the boys for military campaigns. The boys only had a red cloak to wear. They slept outside on mats they made from reeds. They had to scavenge food from the fields or steal from somewhere. If they were caught, they received a whipping. The boys were also ritually flogged each year in the Temple of Artemis to test their endurance and resistance to pain. Some boys died from the abuse.

The third level was the *hebontes.* These young men would range from age twenty to thirty. At this level, the Spartan trainees received hazing from their instructors and the older military men. If they showed any weakness, they were singled out. They lived in military barracks until they were thirty. They ate small and simple meals. Being overweight was considered unpatriotic since it kept a person from fighting well. The young soldiers drank diluted wine, but getting drunk was forbidden. The training was about discipline in all areas. A young man had to complete his training in the agoge to become a citizen.

A bronze figurine of a young Spartan soldier reclining while eating. He is probably eating a bowl of black bean soup, a typical simple meal. [17]

Warfare Tactics Taught to Spartan Boys

Sparta was Greece's leading military power. The other city-states trained their young men in the art of war, but they didn't have a full-time army. The soldiers were farmers, craftsmen, merchants, or administrators when they weren't fighting battles. However, Sparta's men trained for thirteen years before fighting their first battle, and then they trained for another decade. Their only job was serving in the military.

What military skills did they learn in the agoge? They learned hand-to-hand combat, sword fighting, and spear maneuvers. They also studied formation skills. In the Archaic era, Greek armies began using a ***phalanx formation.*** The soldiers lined up side by side. There were about one hundred men in a row. Each man held his shield in his left hand so it slightly overlapped the shield of the man next to him. It was like a solid wall of shields.

The soldiers were called ***hoplites.*** They wore bronze helmets, breast-plates, and shin guards. In their right hands, they carried seven-foot spears. The typical Greek phalanx was eight men deep. The soldiers in the front row held their spears horizontally to spear the enemy. When the commander yelled, "Charge!" the warriors screamed and ran toward the enemy. The men in the back rows rested their shields on the backs of the men in front of them, pushing them along. It was like a massive bulldozer with spears sticking out.

Phalanx formation.[18]

The Spartan warriors put their own spin on the Greek phalanx formation with the *othismos tactic*. This formation only had four rows instead of eight, but it was much wider. This allowed them to get around the sides of the enemy phalanx. Another thing the Spartans did was slowly and steadily march toward the enemy rather than screaming and running at them. The incredibly disciplined Spartan troops held their formation, chanting their battle hymns to the tune of the pipers. It was a threatening sight, and it scared their enemies. Many times, the enemy soldiers fled in fear when the Spartan phalanx approached.

One battle tactic the Spartans occasionally used was running away. This tactic had two versions: walking and running. In the first version, the Spartan officers assessed the situation. Were they hopelessly outnumbered? Were they in a poor position, such as fighting uphill or with the sun in their eyes? If the officers decided they didn't have a good chance of winning, they would simply walk away from the battle. They didn't care if the other Greeks thought it was a cowardly move. The Spartans knew they were not weaklings. They were practical. It made sense to wait until the odds were in their favor.

The other tactic involved running away in a fake retreat. If the battle wasn't going well, the commander would yell, "Retreat!" Everyone would spin around and run away from the enemy. Of course, the enemy would charge after them at full speed. The Spartan commander led his troops to a better position, such as on a slope, where they would have the uphill advantage.

Then, the Spartan commander screamed, "Turn!" All the Spartan troops wheeled around, holding their spears before them. Caught off guard, the enemy soldiers couldn't stop in time and ran right into the Spartan spears. The Spartans used this fake-retreat tactic often, and the enemy almost always fell for it.

What About Spartan Women?

Spartan girls and women were free spirits in the Greek world. Women in the rest of Greece wore head coverings and ankle-length gowns. They weren't involved in public life. Spartan women wore short skirts. They ran races, wrestled, and threw javelins. Spartan girls lived at home, but they attended school, where they learned reading, writing, singing, dancing, and self-defense moves.

A Spartan girl competing in a race.[19]

There was no such thing as a normal home life for young Spartan couples. All Spartan men lived in the military barracks until they were thirty. They married around the age of twenty, but they didn't live with their wives until they were thirty. The young men occasionally snuck out of the barracks to spend a little time with their wives. Much of the time, they were away at war.

The birth rate in Sparta was much lower than in the rest of Greece. Since the men weren't around, the women handled the family finances and decision-making. Spartan women could buy and sell property.

The men in the rest of Greece were shocked to learn that Spartan women had opinions. Spartan women aired their views in public and even discussed politics. And their husbands listened to them! The non-Spartan Greeks found it odd that Spartan law required that parents give their girls the same quality of care and food as they gave their boys.

Helots and Hoplites: An Oppressive System

In the Bronze Age, the Dorian people migrated into the Peloponnese Peninsula from Macedonia. The Dorians grew in strength and rebuilt the city of Sparta in the early Archaic era. As their population grew, they needed more land for farming. To get that land, they started a twenty-year war with the neighboring city-state of Messenia. It all began with a quarrel over cows.

An Olympic athlete from Messenia named Polychares leased land from a Spartan named Euaiphnos. Polychares grazed his cattle on the land. One day, Euaiphnos told Polychares that pirates had stolen his cattle. Polychares thought his story seemed fishy, so he asked around. He discovered Euaiphnos had sold his cattle. He confronted Euaiphnos, who apologized. "I'll give you the money I got from the cattle. Send your boy over later today, and I'll give him the money."

Instead of handing over the money, Euaiphnos murdered Polychares's son. The distraught father charged into the Spartan council, demanding justice. But the council refused to discuss the matter. Outraged, Polychares went on a killing spree. He murdered any Spartans that he caught walking alone. The Spartan council messaged Messenia. The councilors demanded that Polychares stand trial. The Messenians retorted, "Of course! We'll send Polychares to you as soon as you send Euaiphnos to us. He needs to stand trial for murdering Polychares's son!"

The negotiations did not go anywhere. Both sides started bringing up offenses from decades earlier. The two Spartan kings used the dispute as an excuse to launch a surprise attack on Messenia. Although tensions were high, the city-state of Messenia wasn't expecting war. The two city-states had coexisted peacefully for over a century. The Spartans attacked the town of Ampheia at night, killing the unarmed people in their beds. A fierce war raged for two decades. Sparta won in 720 BCE. One of the towns the Spartans conquered was Helos. Its people were called helots.

Sparta took the land it had stolen from Messenia and divided it into nine thousand estates, all the same size. Each Spartan citizen got a plot of land to farm. Since the Spartan men were full-time soldiers and often off fighting wars, who could do the farming? The Spartans used the helots to tend the fields. The helots weren't exactly slaves because no Spartan owned a helot. They couldn't buy and sell helots. Instead, the helots were more like serfs. Technically, the helots belonged to the state and were assigned work. The helots did all the labor and got half of the profit; the Spartan landowners got the other half. This freed up the Spartan men to form the most formidable military in the ancient Greek world.

So, Sparta had a system where the Spartan men worked full time as soldiers, and the helots farmed the land and did other menial work. But what about merchants and artisans? Sparta had a third class called the **Perioikoi.** They were free people, but they came from other places and couldn't be citizens. Only Spartans who could trace their ancestors back for centuries could be citizens. Thus, the Perioikoi couldn't serve in the military. But they could run shops, make pottery and weapons, and engage in trade. The Perioikoi grew wealthy, but they couldn't own land.

5th century BCE statue of a Spartan hoplite.[20]

Everything was working out for the Spartans. Every Spartan citizen owned land, but he didn't have to do the demanding farm work. But a new problem arose. The helot men lived at home with their wives and had large families. The Spartan men were off fighting wars or living in Sparta's military barracks. It wasn't long before the helot population outnumbered the Spartans. What was to keep them from rebelling against Sparta and taking over the city-state?

Plutarch was a 1st-century CE historian. He was also a priest at Apollo's temple in Delphi, where the Oracle was. In his book *Parallel Lives*, Plutarch said the Spartans came up with a devious plan to decrease the helot population. They picked Spartan teens who displayed exceptional skills in the agoge to join a force called the **Krypteia**. It was similar to a secret police. Every autumn, the Spartans declared war on the helots. This meant no Spartan could be found guilty of killing a helot. The young men who joined the Krypteia took a dagger and went into the countryside to find and kill helots.

What Was Sparta's Lasting Legacy?

Spartan culture influenced Western ideas about self-discipline, courage, self-sacrifice, and patriotism. Sparta was light-years ahead of the rest of Greece in terms of women's contributions to society. Women weren't hidden at home. They aired their opinions, were physically strong, and enjoyed rights like buying and managing property. Aristotle said that women owned two-fifths of Sparta's land.

Yet, Sparta had a dark side. The Spartans killed weak or sickly newborns. Spartan men lived apart from their wives and barely saw their children. Children belonged to the state, not to the family. Mothers only cared for their male children for six years. Parents had no say in their children's education or anything else about their lives from that point on. The family breakdown made Sparta militarily strong, but Sparta suffered horrific losses sometimes. At times, almost all of the adult males died. Sparta didn't have enough children to rebuild its population. Then, there were the helots. The Spartans essentially enslaved their neighbors and occasionally murdered some of them when the helot population grew larger than the Spartans.

These Spartan ideals of a strong military and state influenced later societies. The classical Greek philosopher Plato liked how the state controlled children's lives and education. Hitler thought Sparta was a model civilization. German children were taught strict discipline, endurance, and the importance of self-sacrifice. Hitler believed Sparta was a prime example of a warrior class.

Round-up Activity: Review Questions

1. How did Sparta's culture and society differ from other ancient Greek city-states?

2. What role did military service play in Spartan society?

3. What was the agoge? How did it shape the upbringing and education of Spartan boys?

4. What challenges did Spartan boys face in their rigorous training and education?

5. What were some positive aspects of Sparta's legacy?

6. How has Sparta's legacy negatively impacted some civilizations?

Chapter 5: The Persian Wars: Marathon and Thermopylae

For 160 years, the Persian Empire, also known as the Achaemenid Empire, and Greece fought each other. For the first six decades, Persia had the upper hand. But three epic battles turned the tide for Greece. This chapter will unlock the remarkable heroism and canny strategies the Greeks used to achieve victory.

What Caused the Persian Wars?

It all began with Cyrus the Great, King of Persia. His empire was located in what is today southern Iran. He united with his kinsmen, the Medes of northern Iran, and they conquered central Asia. Then, they charged through Turkey, taking more territory, until they arrived in Ionia, across the Aegean Sea from Greece. Shockwaves rippled through the Greek world when Ionia bowed to Persia in 547 BCE. These were colonies settled by Greek city-states centuries before. Now, the Persian-Achaemenid Empire had swallowed them up.

In 499 BCE, the Ionians rebelled during the reign of Persian King Darius the Great. Athens and the neighboring city of Eretria sent ships and troops to the Ionians. They sacked and burned Sardis, the Persian capital of Ionia. In 494, the Persians trounced the Greek army, and the revolt fell apart. Yet, Darius was seething. "How dare Athens and Eretria interfere in my war!"

Darius sent his relative Mardonius overland to Greece, but the bloodthirsty Byrgi tribe blocked his way. Meanwhile, a brutal storm sank three hundred of the Persian ships sailing toward Greece. Darius simmered in rage. He wasn't done with Greece yet!

Inconceivable Victory at Marathon

In 490 BCE, Darius sent his ambassadors to the Greek city-states, demanding they submit to his authority. Most Greek city-states agreed to give "earth and water," meaning they recognized Persia as their overlord. But there were some holdouts. Athens and Sparta refused to yield. Darius roared, "Athens, again? They interfered in Ionia. I won't stop until I burn Athens to the ground."

A fleet of triremes.[21]

When Darius's navy with six hundred *triremes* (warships) sailed across the Aegean Sea toward Greece, the people of Eretria panicked. They had destroyed Sardis in the Ionian revolt. Surely, the Persians would punish them. Most fled to Mount Olympus, where they hid out. The Athenians sent four thousand men, but Eretria's city leader sent them back home. "Our citizens aren't planning to fight the Persians. There's no sense in dying for a lost cause."

As it turned out, two Eretrians opened the city gates to the Persians, hoping for a reward. That didn't go well for them. The Persians killed every man left in the city and enslaved the women and children. They sacked and burned Eretria and destroyed its temples. A few days later, the Persians sailed toward Athens, expecting a similar triumph.

Meanwhile, the Athenians sent a long-distance runner named Philippides to run 132 miles (213 kilometers) to Sparta. When the Spartans heard that the Persians had crushed Eretria, they agreed to help, even though Sparta and Athens were usually bitter rivals. Sparta had some weird religious rules about when they could and could not fight.

"Yes, of course, we'll help. The Persians are probably targeting us next since we didn't give them 'earth and water.' If we join forces, we can beat them. But, right now, we're in the middle of the Carnelian festival. We can't go to war until the full moon."

This news was discouraging, as the Persian ships were on the way. The Athenians brightened when the city of Plataea, north of Athens, sent a thousand warriors to help. The Athenians were still outnumbered, but they had a few tricks up their sleeves. They chose a daring strategy. Instead of letting the Persians lay siege to Athens, they marched across the Attica Peninsula to meet their attackers in Marathon. The Persians weren't familiar with Marathon's landscape, but the Greeks knew it well. Marathon was in a swampy valley. **Quagmire**, soft marshy areas that gave way under a person's weight, covered the area. If a person stepped on it, they got sucked in. Any struggle increased the downward force until the doomed person drowned in the bog.

The Persians had just laid anchor at Marathon when the Greeks showed up. The Persians had planned to ride their horses across the peninsula rather than sailing around the bottom of it. They wanted to avoid the lethal storms in the open sea that had wiped out their fleet earlier. When the Persians saw the Greeks coming over the mountains, they smiled.

"Look! The Greeks don't have any horses! They're all on foot! And they only have spears and swords. Our cavalry and archers will wipe them out!"

This was the first time the Persians faced off against the Greeks in a land battle. The Greeks always fought on foot, using their phalanx maneuvers. The Persians were skilled cavalrymen, and their terrifying archers would darken the sky with arrows. But when the Persians came ashore, they realized they couldn't use their horses on the marshy, mountainous terrain.

The Greeks formed their phalanx position on the mountain while the Persians assembled on the small plain below. The Greeks charged downhill, running full speed, catching the Persians by surprise. The Persian archers barely had time to shoot off two volleys of arrows. Most of the arrows hit helmets or shields and bounced off. The Greeks quickly outflanked and encircled the Persians, confusing them.

Panicked, the Persians ran toward their ships, Greek spears flying into their unprotected backs. They had to navigate through the marshland. Many fell into the quagmire. They finally reached the sea, but the Athenians plunged in after them. The Athenians captured seven Persian ships and set others on fire.

The Greeks attack the Persian ships.[22]

The rest of the Persians hoisted their sails and sailed out to sea. The Greeks joyfully assessed the losses. They counted 6,400 dead Persians.

Who knew how many more had sunk in the quagmire? The Athenians only lost 192 men, and 11 men from Plateau died.

"Look!" someone shouted, pointing out to sea. "The Persians are sailing south! They're not sailing back to Asia! They're headed around the peninsula to Athens!"

The Greek officers hurriedly called the men to order. "We've got to get back to Athens! If our army isn't there when those ships arrive, the people in the city might surrender to the Persians."

Would they make it in time? Athens was twenty-five miles away. Exhausted after the battle, the Greeks raced back, stumbling over roots and rocks in the dim light of the full moon. They got there before the Persians and collapsed at the temple of Heracles on the cliff overlooking the Saronic Gulf. The Persians saw their campfires as they sailed into the gulf. They dropped their anchor and discussed their next move.

Should they lay siege? They had already lost thousands of men and many ships. The Greeks were pumped up by their victory, and other Greek cities, like Sparta, would likely come to help the Athenians. After floating in the gulf for a while, they weighed anchor and sailed over the horizon to Persia. This was when the Spartans finally showed up, as it was now a full moon. But the Athenians embraced them, and they all hurried back to Marathon to see the dead Persians and hear how the battle went down.

The Greeks had scored an outstanding victory, but they knew the Persians would return. One of Athens's generals, Miltiades, had overseen the battle at Marathon. He realized that Athens had to build up a navy that could take on the Persians. General Themistocles heartily agreed. They ordered the construction of two hundred new triremes. From this point, Athens's nearly unbeatable navy ruled the seas.

Spartan Sacrifice at Thermopylae

Darius the Great died soon after. He never realized his dream of conquering Greece. His son Xerxes now stood before the Persian council. "We cannot let Greece get away with this! They have insulted my father and the Persian Empire. I'll build the largest army the world has ever seen. One million men! All of humanity will be under our yoke. Persia will be the empire upon which the sun never sets!"

The men on the council drew in a collective breath but stayed silent. Xerxes had a hot temper, and they wanted to keep their heads. The Persian Empire stretched from Egypt to Afghanistan, so a million-man army was doable. However, Persia had suffered horrific losses in their previous battles with Greece. Finally, Xerxes's uncle, Artabanus, cleared his throat and reminded him of the grave risk. Xerxes was adamant.

"Artabanus, you're a coward! Stay here with the women. We must strike first! Otherwise, they'll invade us!"

The Greek historian Herodotus said that Xerxes had second thoughts while lying on his bed that night. Artabanus was right! Attacking Greece could spell Persia's doom. He drifted asleep. A ghost appeared in his dream. "Are you changing your mind, Persian? Follow your original plan!"

Xerxes awoke the following day, rubbing his head. What a crazy dream! He called his council and apologized to his uncle. He announced that Persia would *not* invade Greece. But that night, the ghost appeared again. "If you don't invade Greece, you will experience a sudden and violent end."

Xerxes jumped up and ran into Artabanus's room. "I keep seeing a ghost. It's insisting I attack Greece. I don't know whether it's real or just my imagination. Why don't you lie on my bed? See what happens."

Artabanus lay down on his nephew's bed. The ghost appeared and tried to gouge out his eyes. "You! You're the one telling Xerxes not to invade Greece! You now face judgment! Judgment now and in the afterlife!"

Artabanus jumped up and ran screaming to Xerxes. "I've changed my mind! Invade Greece!"

After four years of preparation, Xerxes marched his massive army to the Dardanelles, where Asia meets Europe. Instead of simply ferrying his men over the one-mile-wide strait, he decided to do the unthinkable. He would build a bridge! He had his engineers strap 674 ships together and put a path of planks over them. The engineers finished the job, but a storm struck. The wind and churning waters destroyed the bridge.

The boat bridge over the Dardanelles.[23]

Xerxes erupted in anger. He cut the heads off the engineers and ordered his men to punish the water. They branded the water with hot irons and whipped it three hundred times! Now, he had to get new engineers to rebuild the bridge, which meant spending the winter there and using up precious food stores to feed his large army.

Were there really a million soldiers in Xerxes's army? The Persian Empire was the largest the world had yet seen, and they had the manpower. However, all the planning, organization, and food needed for that many men would have made it impractical, if not impossible.

The bridge was eventually rebuilt. Xerxes's army crossed over and marched toward Greece. Meanwhile, his navy of 1,200 ships sailed across the Aegean Sea. None of the city-states of northern Greece dared resist his massive army. But then, the Persian soldiers reached a high and rugged mountain range that cut through Greece. The Persians had to go through the Thermopylae Pass to get to southern Greece. But six thousand Greek warriors barred his way. Sparta had allied with Athens, Thebes, Arcadia, Corinth, and other southern Greek city-states. Some allied Greek forces stayed behind and shored up defenses in southern Greece. Meanwhile, the Spartans and other Greeks blocked the sixteen-foot-wide pass and quickly rebuilt a crumbling defensive wall.

Xerxes chuckled. He believed as soon as the Greeks saw his gigantic army pouring into the valley, they would run away. But he was dealing with Spartans, the best fighters of ancient Greece. After four days of staring at each other, Xerxes sent an ambassador to Spartan King Leonidas. "This is your last chance. Lay down your weapons and avoid bloodshed."

Leonidas growled, "You will have to take them!"

The Greeks put the phalanx formation into play. They stood shoulder to shoulder, their shields overlapping and spears sticking out. The ones in the back held their shields overhead, forming a bronze ceiling that deflected the thousands of arrows shot by the Persians. If one man was hit, another quickly stepped into his place from behind. The ancient defensive wall protected the men on the front line from a cavalry charge.

The Persians only had wicker shields. These were no match for the Greeks' long spears. For two full days, the Greeks blocked the Persians from entering the pass. Xerxes sent his ten thousand "Immortals," Persia's elite forces, to charge forward with their battleaxes, javelins, and swords. Even these great warriors failed. The seven-foot Greek spears kept them from getting close enough to use their own weapons.

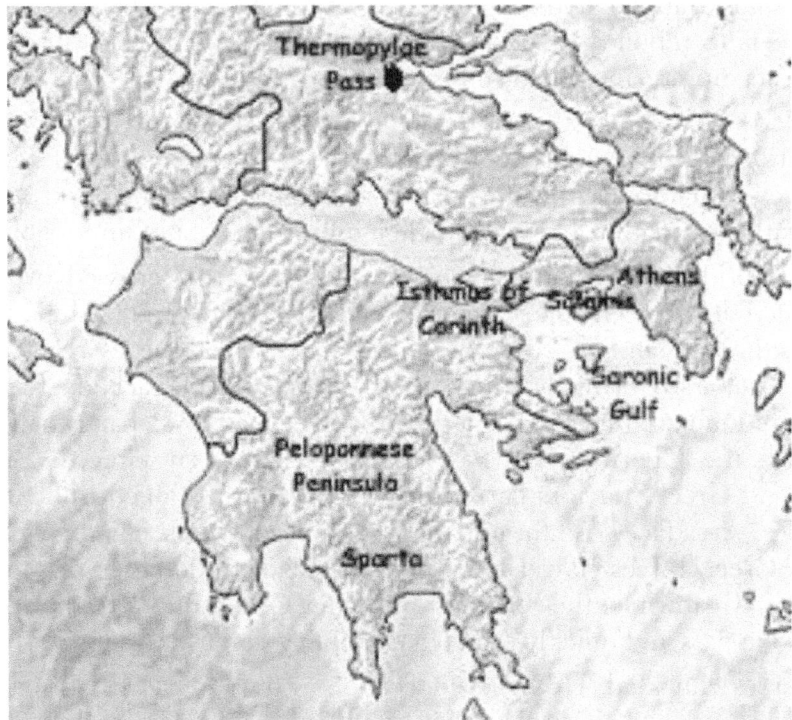

Thermopylae Pass (top of map).[24]

On the third day, a Greek traitor showed the Persians how a few men could get over the mountain on a narrow shepherd's path. Some Immortals scaled the mountain and approached the Greeks from behind. Leonidas ordered a few hundred men to continue holding the line against the Persians. He sent a small unit to attack the Persians who had just crossed the mountain. He ordered the rest of the Greeks to get out of the pass and escape to southern Greece.

There was no way the Greeks could continue to hold the pass with Persians in front and behind them. Why should all six thousand Greeks die when they could live to fight another day? They were desperately needed in southern Greece because Xerxes was headed there next. Leonidas and the small remaining force continued holding off the Persians until more Immortals crossed over the mountain, trapping them in the pass. The Immortals shot volleys of arrows at the Greeks, killing King Leonidas. Soon, every Greek man was dead. The Spartans and their allies sacrificed themselves to save Greece.

Naval Battle at Salamis Turns the Tide

The Persian forces charged south toward Athens, but the city was empty. Most of the citizens evacuated to the island of Salamis. Xerxes looted the city's treasures. He burned its stunning temples and killed anyone he could find. He received the terrible news that two storms had wiped out half his naval fleet. Cursing the gods, he considered his next move.

He couldn't do anything about the Athenians until the rest of his fleet arrived. But he had a score to settle with Sparta. To get there, he needed to cross the Isthmus of Corinth into the Peloponnese Peninsula. However, the Spartans and their Peloponnesian allies were one step ahead of him. While Leonidas and his men held off the Persians at the Thermopylae Pass, the rest of the Greeks had been busy rebuilding an ancient four-mile wall that spanned the Isthmus of Corinth.

When Xerxes laid siege to the newly built wall, the Greeks knew they couldn't hold Xerxes off for very long. They needed to lure the Persians away. The Athenian, Corinthian, and Spartan fleets were moored near Salamis in the Saronic Gulf. The Athenian naval commander Themistocles messaged Xerxes. He convinced Xerxes that the Greek alliance was falling apart and the Spartans were sailing home. Themistocles told Xerxes he was willing to come over to the Persian side. If Xerxes sent his fleet to Salamis the next day, he would give the

Athenian navy to the Persians.

Xerxes fell for it. He sent his fleet to the Saronic Gulf. He headed to the gulf and climbed a mountain to watch the battle play out below him. Most of the Greek ships hid behind Georgios Island in the Saronic Gulf. When the Persian navy entered the gulf, they saw fifty Corinthian ships floating in front of them. Suddenly, the Corinthian ships sailed into the strait between Salamis and Athens on the mainland. The Persian ships followed them into the narrow strait. They realized too late it was a trap!

An illustration of the Battle of Salamis.[25]

The rest of the Greek ships came out of hiding and encircled the Persian fleet. The Persians had no way to escape. The Greeks chanted a hymn to Apollo as they shattered the Persian ships with their battering rams. Floating bodies and sinking ships covered the surface of the water.

Xerxes watched in horror from the mountaintop as the Greeks destroyed his naval fleet. This was the watershed moment for Greece. The tide had turned in the long war with Persia. Greece would ultimately prevail.

Round-up Activity: Fill in the Blank

The Persian Wars with Greece began when Cyrus the Great conquered _____ in 547 BCE, making these Greek colonies a province of the Persian-Achaemenid Empire. When Ionia revolted in 499 BCE, Athens and _____ sent ships and troops to help. After ending the revolt, the Persian king, Darius the Great, sent his fleet to punish Athens. However, the Athenians chose the battleground in a marshy area where the Persians couldn't use their horses. They soundly defeated the Persians in the _____ ____ _____. Xerxes, the son of Darius, sought revenge and marched into Greece with a huge army. Led by the Spartan king _____, the Greeks held off the Persians at the _____ _____ while the rest of the Greeks evacuated _____ and rebuilt the wall at the _____ ____ _____. The Greeks sacrificed themselves at the pass, but in the end, the Greeks scored an astounding victory in the naval _____ ____ _____.

    Athens
    Battle of Marathon
    Battle of Salamis
    Eretria
    Ionia
    Isthmus of Corinth
    Leonidas
    Thermopylae Pass

Chapter 6: The Golden Age of Athens: Art, Philosophy, and Democracy

From 480 to 423 BCE, Athens shone like never before. It made mind-blowing strides in the arts, philosophy, and democracy. What shaped these glory days that left such an imprint on world history? Athens formed the Delian League, uniting the Greek city-states and pushing pirates and Persians out of Greek waters. This relative peace allowed Athens to focus on culture and trade.

Astounding Architecture

Gleaming temples with graceful pillars leap to mind when one thinks of Athens. Like many Greek cities, Athens was centered around a steep hill called an *Acropolis*, or "high city." The Athenians built elegant government and temple buildings on this "Sacred Rock." But when Xerxes stormed Athens with his huge army, he destroyed the Acropolis.

After the Greeks sank Xerxes's navy and sent him scurrying back to Persia, the Athenians began rebuilding. Once the walls were up to protect the city, they built a breathtaking new complex on the Acropolis. A person climbing the Acropolis entered through the marble Propylaea Gate. A thirty-foot-high statue of Athena stood just behind the gate. Ships on the gulf three miles away could see the shining bronze statue reflecting the sun.

Another temple to Athena on the Acropolis was the Erechtheion, which still stands today. It has an unusual type of pillar called *caryatid* on its "Porch of the Maidens." Sculptures of lovely young women support its roof. Each caryatid pillar is different. They might represent real teenagers from ancient times.

Caryatid pillars in the Temple of the Erechtheion.[26]

Impressive Artistry

Around 530 BCE, the Greeks invented a type of pottery called "*red-figure*" or "red-on-black." Artists first painted the pottery black. Then, they painted people or animals in red or gold over the black paint. The earlier style had black figures painted on a red background. One example of this artwork is a painting of a Greek hoplite and a Persian archer on a shiny black amphora jar. The Greek soldier wears a short skirt and bronze armor. The Persian soldier wears long pants and a long-sleeved shirt.

Red-on-black amphora jar.[27]

Another example of a red (or gold) on black ceramic painting is a vase with a singer and a bunny. A bearded man relaxes on a couch under a basket. He is singing and reaching down to pet his spotted rabbit. Have you ever thought of people having bunnies thousands of years ago? The painting is on a *kylix*, a ceramic drinking cup with a wide bowl and horizontal handles.

Singer and bunny.[28]

Another red-on-black vase has a painting of Dionysus, the god of wine. Two *maenads* are dancing on both sides of Dionysus. What were maenads? They were young priestesses who worshiped Dionysus through dance. The word "maenad" means demented or crazy. As these young women danced, Dionysus's spirit possessed them. Don't be fooled by their seemingly harmless appearance! When these women were "under the influence," they developed superpowers and could kill an animal or person with their bare hands.

Dionysus and dancing maenads.[29]

Classical Greek statues had perfect, lifelike bodies. The artist Phidias built an imposing thirty-eight-foot-high statue of Athena for the Parthenon temple on the Acropolis. It had a wooden frame covered by sheets of gold. The goddess's arms and face were ivory. Her statue was eventually destroyed, but its image on Greek coins helps us know what it looked like. The white marble Parthenon temple still sits on the highest point of the Acropolis in Athens.

A life-sized replica of the Athena Parthenos.[30]

Groundbreaking Philosophy

Famous philosophers lived during the Golden Age of Athens. They discussed almost everything. They thought about what was right and wrong. How can a person really know the difference? They also talked about human nature. Were humans more important than animals? How does reason set humans apart from other creatures? They shared their theories on politics, math, science, and many other topics.

Hippias lived in the Peloponnese, but he visited Athens to argue with Socrates and Plato. He was a ***Sophist*** or an expert in wisdom. Plato loved to poke holes in his reasoning. Hippias discussed a wide range of topics, such as art, astronomy, history, math, music, and philosophy. He attended the Olympic Games. Anybody there could ask him to give a speech about any topic. He could speak about just about anything without preparing.

Hippias pointed out that society constantly changes its ideas about right and wrong. Because of this, he reasoned that we can't depend on society to define morality. Instead, he said a ***natural law*** applies to all places and times. This law never changes. What is right is always right, no matter where or when. Evil is always evil. For example, it's always right to help the weak and helpless.

The most famous philosophers from Athens were Socrates, Plato, and Aristotle. Socrates taught Plato, and Plato taught Aristotle. Aristotle taught Alexander the Great, who conquered much of the known world. Socrates never told his students what to think. Instead, he asked questions. He wanted them to think for themselves. Socrates admitted that he did not know everything. He knew he didn't have all the answers. He called this "simple ignorance." Socrates said this was better than clueless people who claimed to have all the answers. He called this "double ignorance."

Socrates said that an unexamined life is not worth living. What is an unexamined life? Some people live life thinking they already know everything they need to know. They are not interested in learning new things. Other people know that they have only tapped the surface of knowledge. An entire world is out there to explore. In their eyes, a worthy life is spent doing that.

Socrates faced trial on charges of impiety and corrupting Athens's youth. ***Impiety*** means "godlessness." The authorities said that Socrates did not believe in the gods of Athens. Socrates was not an ***atheist*** (someone who does not believe in a higher power). He did believe in his own god. However, he pointed out that the Greek gods were constantly cheating on their spouses, stealing things, and lying. They set a bad example for people to follow. The city leaders said that Socrates believed in "new spiritual things," and he did. His god was perfect, wise, and moral. By introducing this new idea of god and criticizing the Greek gods, Socrates was found guilty of leading young people away from the true religion. He was forced to commit suicide by drinking hemlock poison.

Socrates had to drink hemlock for corrupting Athens's youth.[31]

Plato taught that what we see around us isn't actual reality. He said it's like we're all living in a cave. The sun is outside, but we can't see the sun. All we can see are the shadows the sun casts into the cave. In his *Theory of Forms*, Plato said that philosophy was about understanding that something outside was causing these shadows. There's more to life than the cave. True reality is outside the cave, where there is sunshine, blue skies, and fresh air. If a person could escape from the cave, they could see that a better world is out there.

Plato's student Aristotle talked about the perfect, eternal, **unmoved mover**, who set everything into motion. He said this being brought order into the world. Aristotle came to this conclusion through deduction. What is **deduction**? Aristotle said that if "premises," or ideas, about something are true, we can "deduce" or come to the correct conclusion.

For example, let's say we have the idea or premise that all kangaroos are mammals. Our second premise is that all mammals are warm-blooded. Our conclusion is that all kangaroos are warm-blooded. But what if we exchange kangaroos for elephants? Both premises would still be true. Elephants are mammals; thus, they are warm-blooded. But can we exchange elephants for jellyfish? No, because they aren't mammals. Both premises have to be true for a correct conclusion. Aristotle used this understanding of deduction to move on to *induction*, which uses known facts to assume universal or well-known truths.

Developments in Democracy

All these philosophical discussions led to innovative ideas about democracy. That brings us to Pericles, who brought Athens to new political heights. In fact, the Golden Age of Athens is sometimes called the "Age of Pericles." He transformed Athens's government system into "the rule of the many instead of the few." His vision was to write a constitution that other Greek city-states could follow. Under Pericles's "radical democracy," everyone had equal justice by law. It didn't matter whether they were poor or lower class. They had the same rights. Well, the men did, at least. Women had few rights and had to depend on someone to represent them in court.

Pericles.[32]

Pericles said the middle and lower classes should serve in government positions. He even paid for jury service so working-class citizens could take time off from their jobs to participate in the court system. Previously, only the wealthy served as city administrators because everyone else had to work. Now, city officials got paid so that anyone could do the job.

The Delian League Ejects the Persians and Pirates

After most of southern Greece's city-states allied to squash Xerxes and his Persian invasion, they realized that cooperation was the key to keeping the Persians away forever. The Athenian colonies in Ionia revolted again. This time, they were successful. The allied Greek navy conquered part of Thrace on Greece's northeastern border. In 478 BCE, they captured Byzantium on the Bosporus Strait between Europe and Asia. Centuries later, Roman Emperor Constantine rebuilt Byzantium. He renamed it Constantinople, and it served as the capital of the Eastern Roman Empire.

With these victories, the Greeks controlled the Aegean Sea. At this point, Sparta was ready to withdraw from allied warfare. Sparta always had an independent streak. Plus, they were concerned about Ionia, which was just next to Persia's territory. They didn't think protecting Ionia was possible. They suggested moving all the Ionian Greeks to mainland Greece. This idea infuriated the Ionians, who had lived there for hundreds of years. The Athenians said, "They're our colonies. We can protect them ourselves!"

In 478 BCE, the Athenians took over the Delian League. This was the Greek alliance of Ionia and other islands and coastal cities in the Aegean Sea. The league's first naval commander was Cimon. He had fought in Marathon and Salamis against the Persians. The 330 cities that belonged to the alliance provided warships or money in the war against the Persian-Achaemenid Empire.

Meanwhile, the Persians assembled another enormous army and navy to attack Greece again. But Cimon struck first in a land and sea battle at Pamphylia in today's western Turkey. He sunk two hundred Persian ships and chased off their army. The Persians stayed out of the Aegean Sea for the next fifteen years. Cimon also drove the Dolopian pirates out of the Aegean, ensuring peaceful trade that enriched the Greeks.

After a successful battle in the north Aegean, Cimon and his Greek allies captured many prisoners. They also gained gold jewelry and priceless purple robes. Cimon asked the allies if they wanted the loot or the prisoners. "Choose whatever you want, and I'll take the other."

"Ha! These prisoners are all upper class. They've never worked a day in their lives. They'll be no good as slaves. We'll take the gold and the robes. You can have them."

So, Cimon took the prisoners. It wasn't long before their affluent families and friends paid Cimon money to free them. He put some money in the Delian League's treasury. He used some to support his navy and used the rest to host meals for the poor in his home.

Egypt had been an unwilling part of the Persian Empire. It revolted in 460 BCE. Pericles sailed 250 Greek ships to aid Egypt against the Persians. The Greeks suffered a devastating loss of twenty thousand men and most of their fleet. This disaster prompted Pericles to move the Delian League's treasury to Athens for "safekeeping." The payments from the city-states went to Athens. Pericles spent it on his building projects on the Acropolis. Athens was now an empire. Yes, the city-states grumbled. Some even tried to pull out of the Delian League, but they were severely punished by Pericles.

Pericles captured the island of Cyprus in the northeastern Mediterranean, but the Persians took it back. In 451 BCE, Cimon sailed with two hundred ships to reclaim Cyprus. He died in the battle, but his officers kept his death a secret until they won the battle. Greece and Persia signed the Callias Treaty, which brought thirty years of peace. The Persians promised to leave Ionia alone and to stay out of the Aegean Sea. The Greeks returned Cyprus to the Persians and promised not to interfere in North Africa or Turkey.

Round-up Activity: You're a Greek Artist!

Below is a blank amphora vase. Use your creativity and imagination to design a picture on the vase. Review the scenes in the book so far for inspiration. Greek vase decorations included battles, everyday life, and Greek deities. You might want to color the picture in gold or red and the background in black.

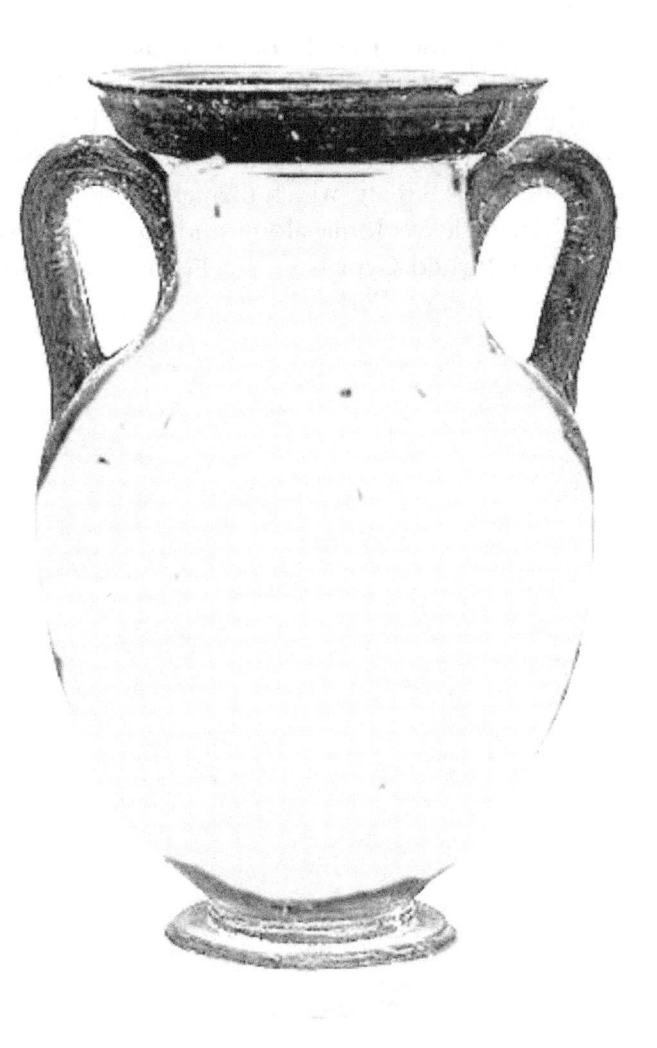

Chapter 7: The Peloponnesian War

For twenty-six years, Athens and Sparta were at each other's throats. It wasn't the first time the two great forces had clashed. An earlier conflict, sometimes called the First Peloponnesian War, raged for fifteen years. Sparta was an unbeatable war machine. Athens had the Delian League's unparalleled naval force. Who would win? The Athenian general Thucydides wrote an eyewitness account in his *History of the Peloponnesian War*.

What Caused the First War? (460–445 BCE)

It all started with a helot uprising. Sparta was stirring up trouble even before that, though. After chasing off the Persians, the Athenians started rebuilding their city. Strangely, Sparta told them not to rebuild the city walls.

"Those crazy Spartans! Why would we leave Athens unprotected? They're up to something!"

The Athenians were right. The Spartans were planning to invade Athens. But two disasters distracted the Spartans. An earthquake occurred, killing thousands. Shortly after, the helots revolted. The Spartans sent word to all their allies, asking for help. Athens was still an ally then. After all, they had fought side by side against Persia. But when Athens sent four hundred men, the Spartans sent them back home.

The Athenians were offended. "Really? They took everyone else's help but not ours? Do they think we'd fight on the helots' side?"

The Spartans finally got the helots under control. But what would keep them from rebelling again? It was time for them to leave! The Spartans kicked them off the Peloponnese Peninsula, which dramatically changed Sparta's structure. Now, not all its men could serve full-time in the army. Somebody needed to stay home and do the farming. The Athenians inserted themselves into the situation by resettling the helots at Naupaktos (today's Nafpaktos) on a narrow strait where the Ionian Sea flows into the Gulf of Corinth. That meant the helots controlled the region's sea trade and ships.

Key cities in the Peloponnesian War.[33]

What Happened in the First War?

The Athenians knew they would soon come to blows with Sparta. They had the Delian League, but they needed to cement other partnerships. They allied with Argos and Megara, which were located between Sparta and Athens. These cities were strategic for controlling the Saronic Gulf and the Isthmus of Corinth. But Megara and Corinth were at war. If Athens allied with Megara, it would get sucked into the war. This conflict began the First Peloponnesian War in 460 BCE.

Athens fought on two fronts at the same time. It helped Libya and Egypt in their attempt to leave the Persian Empire. After sending two hundred ships to North Africa, Athens was short of men and ships to fight Corinth. Athens lost the land wars but scored a victory when its navy captured seventy Peloponnesian warships. When Corinth attacked Megara, most of the Athenian soldiers were at sea. The elderly men and young boys of Athens formed a small army and marched to aid Megara. They won the battle!

Sparta initially stayed out of the fray. It only got involved to help the city of Doris fight Phocis. Both towns were near the helots' new location at Naupaktos, and Sparta wanted friends in the area. The Spartans beat Phocis, but the Athenian navy blocked their way back to the Peloponnese. The enraged Spartans marched toward Athens. The Athenians tried to stop them at Boeotia, but they lost the battle. Sparta also took a brutal hit. The Spartans decided not to attack Athens and headed home.

Athens's navy came into play at this point. It sailed around the Peloponnese Peninsula and attacked its coastal towns. Sparta had never built a navy, so it could not fight the Athenians at sea. To the Spartans' relief, the Persians scored a stunning victory in Egypt, destroying Athens's fleet there. Athens quickly agreed to the Thirty Years' Peace with Sparta and its Peloponnesian allies. However, the peace would only last half that time.

What Started the Second War? (431–404 BCE)

The Corinthians sparked the breakdown in the Thirty Years' Peace. They had a falling out with their colony of Corcyra in northern Greece. When the Corinthians began to build a naval fleet with its Peloponnesian allies, Corcyra begged Athens for help. Athens sent a small fleet to Corcyra. The commander had strict instructions, though. "You're only there to protect Corcyra. Do not attack the Corinthian fleet! If you do, you will break the Thirty Years' Peace."

The Athenian commander couldn't resist launching an attack. He assumed it would be an easy win. It wasn't. Athens had to send more ships to save the day. Meanwhile, other city-states in northern Greece had become increasingly dissatisfied with the Delian League. They were sending a lot of money to Athens and not seeing any benefits. What's worse, the Athenians were bossing them around, telling them how to run their cities.

Corinth thought the time was ripe to get the upper hand over Athens. The Corinthians visited the Spartans to see if they could stir things up. The Athenians heard about it and crashed the party. The old men of the Spartan assembly scowled as the Corinthian and Athenian delegates traded jabs. Then, the Corinthians challenged the Spartans. "You're too passive! If you don't act soon, you'll be surrounded by Athenians!"

The Athenians jumped in, saying, "You'll lose if you break the Thirty Years' Peace. You don't even have a navy! And we have the best navy in the world!"

The Spartans replied, "The way we see it, you Athenians have already broken the treaty. War is on the table!"

General Thucydides of Athens tried calming the hotheads down, "My brothers! Think! War is unpredictable. Count the cost before committing to war. The longer a war lasts, the more things can go wrong. Everyone does war the wrong way around. They leap into action without thinking. It is only after suffering that they begin to think."

Thucydides.[34]

The Second War Begins

By this point, Megara had fallen out with Athens and allied with Sparta. Athens set up a blockade, keeping ships from delivering grain to Megara. Megara asked Sparta for help. The Spartans and Athenians ended up fighting outside Megara's walls. Athens had never won a land battle against Sparta's fierce army. It didn't win this one either. The Athenians left, but Sparta took the war to Athens.

The Siege of Athens

The Spartans surrounded Athens and stole all the produce from the farms around Athens. But General Pericles brought the rural people inside the city, warning everyone not to fight the Spartans. That would be suicidal. He ordered grain from Ionia and Egypt to feed the people. Meanwhile, the Athenian navy blocked any ships from reaching the Peloponnese. Sparta and its allies could not get grain or supplies.

A Horrifying Plague Strikes Athens

The Athenians were receiving plenty of grain shipments. They had enough food. However, the ships brought something else: the plague! Rats on the ships probably carried it. Thucydides got the plague. He was one of the few who recovered. It caused diarrhea, vomiting, and lung infection. People went blind. Their fingers and toes turned black and fell off. The plague killed one-third of the Athenians, including Pericles.

No one knew much about how disease spread in those days. Thucydides noticed that if the vultures ate the dead people, the birds died. He also observed that if someone got the plague and recovered, they didn't get it again. An upside to the plague was that once the Spartans heard about it, they raced away from Athens as fast as their legs could carry them. The people in the Peloponnese peninsula didn't get the plague. The Athenian blockade had kept ships from reaching the peninsula.

The Peace of Nicias

The plague eventually ended, and Athens slowly recovered its strength. The Athenians built forts around the Peloponnese, and its navy resumed attacking the coastal towns. One day, the Spartans attacked an Athenian fort, Pylos. The Athenians beat the Spartans this time! That had never happened before in a land battle. The Athenians were hopeful they could win the war.

That hope turned to worry when the Spartans marched to Thrace. They conquered Athens's colony of Amphipolis, which had silver mines. The angry Athenians exiled General Thucydides for not getting to

Thrace in time. General Cleon of Athens and General Brasidas of Sparta died in the Battle of Amphipolis. Athens and Sparta were tired of fighting and agreed to stop the war.

Athens and Sparta formed the fifty-year Peace of Nicias. They exchanged prisoners of war and returned most of the territories they had taken from each other. The peace treaty only lasted six years. The rest of the Peloponnesian cities wanted nothing to do with it. They formed a separate alliance and attacked Sparta. Sparta defeated the rebels and forced them to join the Peloponnesian League.

The Sicilian Expedition

General Alcibiades was Athens's young and handsome new star. He was a con man. When Sparta's ambassadors came to Athens to hash out the details of the Peace of Nicias, he snatched power. He targeted Syracuse in Sicily. Sicily is the island at the toe of Italy's boot. Syracuse was one of the world's richest cities. It was allied with Sparta at that time.

Indigenous people lived in Sicily long before the Greeks set up colonies there. Segesta was a small indigenous city under attack by the city-state of Selinus, located on Sicily's western coast. Selinus had close ties to Syracuse and Sparta. Segesta begged Athens to help. Athens was happy to help. Maybe they could conquer Syracuse in the process. The Sicilian Expedition set sail in 415 BCE with 284 ships and 6,300 soldiers. They were led by generals Alcibiades, Lamachus, and Nicias.

Ship route from Athens to Syracuse.[35]

As the fleet approached Sicily, the three generals discussed their strategy. Nicias wanted a moderate approach. "We'll stop Selinus's attack on Segesta, sail around Sicily so everyone can see the size of our fleet, and then head home."

Alcibiades thought Nicias's plan didn't go far enough. "We should ally with the Ionian-Greek cities on Sicily. Together, we can take Syracuse!"

Lamachus had an even bolder plan. "Syracuse isn't expecting us. We should sail to Syracuse first and capture the city before they know what's happening!"

After arguing a bit, the generals agreed to do Alcibiades's plan. That didn't go well. The Ionian Greeks didn't want to attack Syracuse. Then, a ship arrived from Athens. Its captain grabbed Alcibiades. "You're coming with us to Athens. You need to stand trial!"

Back in Athens, someone had damaged a number of statues of the god Hermes. Alcibiades was blamed. He boarded the ship but escaped when it got to Italy. Angry at Athens, he turned traitor and offered his services to the Spartans. They welcomed his insider knowledge of Athens.

The Weird Battle of the Walls

When Alcibiades told the Spartans about the Athenian plan to take Syracuse, Sparta sailed its brand new navy to Sicily. Meanwhile, the Athenians had begun a siege of Syracuse. But they had lost the element of surprise. Syracuse quickly built a new wall to protect the city. Then, the Athenians started building a wall to block Syracuse from its harbor. Realizing their plan, the Syracusans began building a counter-wall going directly from the city to the harbor. Both sides raided the other's wall to keep it from going up.

During one raid, the Syracusans killed General Lamachus, leaving only Nicias in control. Nicias had trouble deciding what to do. He wasted a lot of time. He didn't finish the wall blocking the harbor before Sparta's ships arrived. When Sparta's fleet landed with 2,700 men, Nicias decided to launch a sea battle. That didn't go well.

Just when Nicias decided to sail back to Athens, a lunar eclipse happened. Nicias was very superstitious. He visited a soothsayer (someone who predicts the future by consulting supernatural beings or using intuition and logic). The soothsayer told Nicias the eclipse meant he should wait twenty-seven days before doing anything. The delay was fatal. The Syracusan and Spartan fleets trapped the Athenian ships in the harbor and sank them. They surrounded the Athenians' land army, killing thousands of men. They imprisoned the rest. Most of the men starved to death.

The Third Wave

After Athens's devastating loss in Sicily, Sparta launched a fierce assault on Decelea, which was just north of Athens. This cut off supplies from northern Greece. Sparta also retook Athens's silver mines in Thrace. Syracuse sent a fleet to Greece, and the Persians built more ships for Sparta. They wanted Greece to tear itself apart. The Persians also retook Ionia. To make matters worse, Athens experienced a political revolt and rejected democracy. Athens's navy refused to acknowledge the new leadership.

Alcibiades switched sides again when King Agis of Sparta discovered he was having an affair with his wife. Athens's navy made him its new admiral. Alcibiades was a good commander. He led the Athenian navy to an incredible victory in 410 BCE. He crushed the fleets of Sparta and Syracuse. He also took back Ionia. The Athenians were so happy that they embraced democracy again.

Alcibiades.[36]

But then, Alcibiades lost a battle to the Spartans in Ephesus on Turkey's western shore. Athens voted him out as general. Athens executed six other generals. Although they had sunk seventy Spartan ships, a sudden storm kept them from rescuing their own men.

Without Alcibiades and these other experienced generals, the Athenian navy was crippled. Sparta dominated the Aegean Sea and the Dardanelles. The Spartans cut off grain shipments from the Black Sea to Athens. When Athens sailed out to confront the Spartan navy, they suffered a loss at the Battle of Aegospotami. They lost 168 ships and 4,000 sailors.

Outcomes

Without a navy, the war was over for Athens. The city and its allies surrendered in 404 BCE. They had to take down the city walls and give their remaining warships to Sparta. They no longer had city-states sending tribute. Sparta replaced Athens with its own empire. It placed its own governors and military posts in cities throughout Greece. Sparta ejected democracy. It enforced its *oligarchy* system (rule by elders) throughout Greece.

Round-up Activity: True or False?

Can you tell which statements are true and which are false? Check your answers in the back of the book.

1. Homer gave an eyewitness account of the Peloponnesian War. ( )
2. The Athenians resettled the helots at Naupaktos. ( )
3. Athens also fought in North Africa during the first war. ( )
4. Thucydides thought going to war was a great idea. ( )
5. The plague didn't kill many people in Athens. ( )
6. The fifty-year Peace of Nicias only lasted six years. ( )
7. The war moved to Sicily when Athens agreed to help Segesta. ( )
8. General Nicias made quick and sound decisions that won the war in Sicily. ( )
9. Alcibiades switched sides to Sparta and then back to Athens again. ( )
10. Athens won the final Battle of Aegospotami against Sparta. ( )

Chapter 8: Alexander the Great

Who could have guessed that little-known Macedonia would conquer all of Greece? Who would have thought that a united Macedonian-Greek army would wipe out the Persian Empire? Alexander and his father, Philip, were men with big dreams. They had the courage and skill to chase those dreams. And those dreams came true. Alexander ruled an empire covering three continents.

King Philip's Conquests

Macedonia was a large but poor nation north of Greece. Philip II's father was the king. Philip was the youngest of his father's three sons. When Philip's father died, his oldest brother, Alexander II, became king (not to be confused with Alexander the Great). Thebes rose to power over Greece and its neighbors. General Pelopidas forced King Alexander to ally with Thebes. Alexander had to send his youngest brother Philip as a hostage to Thebes. This was to make sure Alexander stayed loyal to Thebes.

Ptolemy, Philip's mother's lover, murdered Alexander so he could take control of the throne. Although the middle brother, Perdiccas, was officially king, he was too young to rule. Ptolemy ruled as his regent (adult representative ruler) until Perdiccas grew up and killed him. In the meantime, Philip II lived in Thebes as a hostage. He was well treated and schooled in Theban military arts.

Perdiccas died in battle, so Philip II became king. Philip wanted to be the ruler of the world's greatest empire. He invented a new weapon, the *sarissa*, a spear three times longer than a man. With his unbeatable army and deadly sarissas, he set out to achieve his dream. Philip captured today's Albania, Bulgaria, Serbia, and Kosovo. He invaded Thrace, grabbed Athens's silver mines, and took control of central Greece.

Alexander and Aristotle

Alexander III (Alexander the Great) was the son of Philip's fourth wife, Olympias. Philip hired Aristotle to teach Alexander when he was thirteen. The famous philosopher taught Alexander ethics, politics, and logical thinking. Alexander found these skills helpful when making quick judgments. They also helped him when he had to set up a government in his new empire.

Aristotle gave Alexander many of the Greek classics to read. Alexander's favorite book was the *Iliad*, the story of the Trojan War. He read it a lot. It was practical information that Alexander could apply to warfare. Alexander couldn't get enough of the stories of Achilles, who became his role model. When he led his army to northwestern Turkey, he stopped at the ruins of ancient Troy to honor Achilles's grave.

The Art of War

Aristotle taught Alexander how to think, but his father taught him how to fight. Alexander learned to ride a horse and fight when he was a child. When Alexander was sixteen, Philip put him in charge of Macedonia when he went to war. Alexander had to fend off rebel tribes in his father's absence. Both of them often went to war together. Sometimes, Philip sent his teenage son to lead an army on his own.

When Alexander was eighteen, he and Philip fought the Battle of Chaeronea against Thebes, Corinth, and Athens. Philip was on the right side of the Macedonian army facing Athens. Alexander commanded the left against Thebes. Other Macedonian officers fought the Corinthians in the middle. The Greek military stretched for three miles. Alexander destroyed the Thebans. Philip and his other generals beat Athens and Corinth.

Macedonia's victory convinced the Greeks to join the Macedonians. In 337 BCE,

Philip II of Macedonia.[37]

Greece's city-states united with Macedonia in the League of Corinth. They swore not to fight each other so they could fight Persia together. Philip would be their commander in chief. Philip's first move was to send General Parmenion across the Aegean Sea with ten thousand soldiers. His orders were to free the Greek city-states in Ionia from Persian rule.

Persian Poison

Meanwhile, the Persian Empire was in chaos. The Persian kings had many wives and concubines. Concubines were sexual partners of the king and other men of high status. They were usually foreign women and not official wives. Concubines generally held a servant status, but some achieved a fairly high standing through palace intrigues.

Because of their many wives and concubines, Persian kings often had one hundred children or more. One king, Artaxerxes III, killed eighty of his half-brothers in one day shortly after he came to the throne. He didn't want any of them to lead a revolt against him. Several years later, his chief officer Bagoas poisoned him and any other royal males who survived the earlier purge.

With all the royal males dead, Bagoas introduced a young man to the court. "This is Darius III. He's the great-grandson of Darius the Great!"

Darius III had served as governor of Armenia. He was also the royal postmaster. Nothing had prepared him to lead an empire. Bagoas wanted Darius to be a figurehead so Bagoas could run things. Darius didn't want Bagoas to be in control. So, Bagoas decided to poison him too. But then, Darius handed Bagoas his cup of wine. "Drink a toast to me!"

Bagoas took the cup, trembling. He knew it had poison in it, but what could he do? With Bagoas dead, Darius could focus on defending his empire against the Macedonian-Greek threat.

Unexpected Murder

In Macedonia, King Philip threw a wedding for his daughter. As he entered the banquet hall, his bodyguard and jealous former lover shoved a dagger between his ribs. Philip collapsed to the floor in a pool of blood. The Macedonian nobility looked in horror at their dead king. Philip only had three sons. Arrhidaeus was *cognitively* (mentally) challenged. Caranus was still a baby. Macedonia's generals surrounded Alexander and crowned him as their new king.

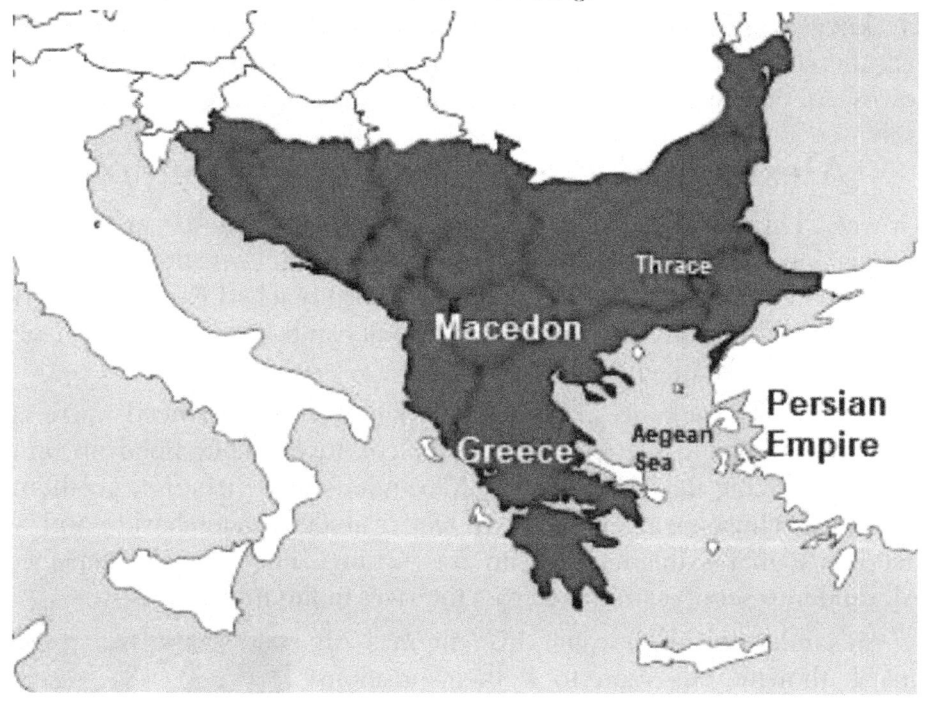

Philip ruled most of the Balkan Peninsula at the time of his murder.[38]

Reconquering Greece

After hearing of Philip's death, Athens and Thebes dropped out of the League of Corinth. Thessaly, Thrace, and Corinth followed their lead. Other cities considered their options. The Macedonians' planned Persian Empire takeover was in trouble.

Alexander marched to northern Greece. The Theban army was waiting for him at the Mount Olympus pass. Alexander took them by surprise. He took a different way around the mountain at night. When he showed up at the Thebans' rear the following morning, he caught them off guard. They immediately surrendered.

Alexander marched into southern Greece, where Athens and Corinth met him apologetically. The Greeks there assured him they would rejoin the league. Alexander turned north. His next target was Thrace. It took a year to make Thrace submit.

Meanwhile, Athens and Thebes had backed out again. Alexander was exasperated and tired of this game. He had spared them the first time. He knew he needed to set an example of what happens to rebels. He hammered Thebes, enslaved its people, and gave its farmland to nearby towns. Athens begged for mercy. Alexander gave it.

Alexander Takes on the Persian Empire

Greece, Thrace, and Macedonia were together again. It was time to pounce on Persia! In 334 BCE, Alexander and forty thousand men crossed the Dardanelles into Asia. When word reached King Darius III, he shrugged and stayed in his palace. "What can this twenty-two-year-old do? My generals will chase him off."

The Persian generals in western Turkey were experienced warriors. They chose their battlefield at the Granicus River. They lined up on a cliff overlooking the river, forcing Alexander's army to come to them. The swift, churning river was sixty feet (eighteen meters) wide and as deep as a man's thigh. The sun was setting. The Persians expected Alexander to set up camp and cross the river in the morning.

Alexander loved to catch his enemies off guard, though. His men took their positions quickly. His elite infantry, with spears three times as long as a man, set up their phalanx position in the center. Alexander led his Macedonian horsemen on the right. His other cavalry lined up on the left. They were guided by an experienced general named Parmenion.

Alexander led the charge as the sky turned black with Persian arrows. His cavalry galloped across the river and climbed the steep bluff. This distracted the Persians and allowed the Greek infantry to wade across the river.

As Alexander's horse reached the top of the steep bank, Alexander thrust his spear into Mithridates, King Darius's son-in-law. But the battleax of a Persian governor, Spithridates, came crashing down on Alexander's helmet, breaking it in half. Miraculously, Alexander was not seriously hurt. His best friend, Black

Alexander, sculpted in the 3rd century BCE by Menas.[39]

Cleitus, speared Spithridates.

By this point, the rest of Alexander's army was crossing the river. They clawed their way up the bluff. When they reached the top and moved into formation with twenty-foot-spears, the Persians' knees buckled under them. They had never faced off against a Greek phalanx. They had never seen such long spears. The panicked Persians raced off the battlefield.

After this victory, the Ionian cities under Persian control surrendered. Alexander attacked the ports of Miletus and Halicarnassus, paralyzing the Perian navy. As he passed through Phrygia, someone pointed out the Gordian Knot. "They say King Midas tied this. Anyone who can untie it will be the ruler of all Asia!"

Alexander inspected the knot. It actually consisted of multiple knots all tangled together. Alexander frowned. Then, he grinned. "Ruler of all Asia, you say?"

He pulled his sword and sliced the knot in two. "Done!"

Darius Runs Away

"Idiots!" King Darius growled. "They ran off the battlefield! I'll have to lead the next battle myself."

Alexander's army marched south along the Mediterranean coast, near Turkey's border with Syria. Without warning, Darius and his army surprised them from behind. They trapped the Greeks between the mountains and sea at the Pinarus River. But Alexander's men knew the drill. They fell into formation like clockwork. They used the same tried-and-true positions as in the previous battle.

The Persians used Greek mercenaries to fight for them. Darius's Greek forces were in the center. Darius's cavalry was by the sea. His Persian foot soldiers stretched along the river into the foothills.

Some Persian foot soldiers crossed the river. They wanted to draw out the Macedonian cavalry. Meanwhile, the Persian cavalry charged over the river, crashing into General Parmenion's cavalry on the left side.

Alexander led a cavalry charge on the right wing. His men broke up the Persian infantry. However, his foot soldiers in the center were getting stuck in the swift river. They couldn't move with their heavy shields and long sarissas. They did not dare to go deeper. When Alexander glanced over and saw his infantry pulling back from the river, he charged directly toward King Darius's chariot. When Darius saw Alexander racing toward him, he wheeled his chariot around and raced off the battlefield. When his men saw their king run away, they looked at each other, wondering what to do. One glance at the Greek horses charging their way settled the matter. They ran off at full speed with the Greeks in hot pursuit.

King Darius III from a mosaic in Pompeii.[40]

Darius was so panicked that he left his mother, pregnant wife, and two daughters behind. The Persians had a habit of taking their women along when they went to war. Alexander took the women and girls with him. He treated them kindly. When the queen died in childbirth, he honored her with a royal funeral. After conquering the empire, Alexander married Stateira II, one of Darius's daughters.

Alexander's army marched south. All the Phoenician cities on Lebanon's coast surrendered. Ancient Tyre was the only holdout. The city was on an offshore island and surrounded by high walls. For seven long months, Alexander tried to break into the city. He built a causeway to the island, but ships from Tyre constantly attacked the workers. Finally, the Ionian Greeks, the other Phoenicians, and the people of the island of Cyprus offered their ships. Alexander attacked Tyre with a fleet of 220 ships and took the city. He crucified two thousand men and enslaved the rest.

Egypt had spent centuries trying to get rid of the Persians. The Egyptians cheered as Alexander marched in. They crowned him their new pharaoh and turned over the royal treasury. Alexander built the city of Alexandria on the Mediterranean coast. Alexandria became the capital of Egypt. It was a key naval base and a bustling center of **Hellenistic** (Greek) artists, scientists, philosophers, and religious leaders.

May I Have My Women Back?

While Alexander was in Egypt, Darius wrote him, asking him to return his mother and daughters. "I'll give you half my empire, a fortune in gold, and one of my daughters in marriage."

Alexander chuckled. "I have both daughters, and I don't plan to stop until I have the whole empire."

The two kings faced off at the Battle of Gaugamela in northern Iraq. This time, Darius had war elephants and scythed chariots. The chariots had three-foot blades sticking out from the wheel hubs. They could cut a man's leg off. However, the Macedonian phalanx was highly flexible. The infantry simply moved over to let the chariots pass.

King Darius was in the center of his army. Alexander led his cavalry around the side. They outflanked the Persians and drew them out from the center. Darius panicked and raced off, followed by his men. He tried to regroup, but one of his governors murdered him, ending the Persian-Achaemenid Empire.

Battle of Gaugamela.[41]

Cultural Interchange

Alexander marched south and entered Babylon. He respected the Middle Eastern culture and began dressing like the locals. His Greek and Macedonian men thought this was a bit odd. They felt he'd gone too far when he started requiring them to bow down and kiss the ground. Babylon became Alexander's headquarters, and he made plans to restore it to its former glory.

Alexander appointed leaders to oversee all the provinces and cities he conquered. He kept most of the same rulers in place. All they had to do was pledge their loyalty to him. He founded dozens of cities named Alexandria. They became hubs for a new cultural fusion of Greek and Middle Eastern ways.

On to the Indian Subcontinent!

Alexander headed to the eastern border of the Persian Empire at the Jaxartes River in today's Tajikistan. He conquered the nomadic tribes of Central Asia. On the way, he captured Roxana, a beautiful princess of the Sogdian people, and married her. When Alexander reached the Jaxartes River, he kept going. He crossed the Hindu Kush mountains into Pakistan. But his soldiers had been away from home for ten years. They were worn out. They wanted to be with their families. So, they refused to take another step east.

Sudden Death and Split Empire

Alexander had no choice but to return to Babylon. He threw a wedding. Eighty Persian princesses married his officers. He married two princesses on the same day: Darius III's daughter and Artaxerxes III's daughter. Soon after hearing the thrilling news that his first wife, Roxana, was pregnant, he became ill. He died at the age of thirty-two. He had never lost a battle.

Alexander's unexpected death plunged the new empire into confusion. He had no chosen heirs. Was Roxana's unborn child a boy or a girl? Who should rule now? How could one person rule three continents? Finally, his generals decided to divide the empire among themselves. Roxana's child (if it was a boy) and Alexander's cognitively challenged brother Arrhidaeus would be joint kings. General Perdiccas would be regent. The generals each took a section of the empire to govern. However, their plans fell apart within months.

Alexander followed in his father's footsteps. He successfully united Greece. Alexander even conquered the world's superpower of his day. He ranks as one of history's most successful military commanders. His military tactics are still studied today. By the age of thirty-two, he had created the largest empire the world had yet seen. Alexander's conquests spread the Greek-Hellenistic culture across his new empire, starting the Hellenistic Age, an era of astonishing scientific and artistic advances.

Round-up Activity: Quiz

1. In what ways did Alexander's upbringing and education influence his leadership style and approach to warfare?

2. What were some of the key military tactics that Alexander the Great used in his conquests? How did these tactics contribute to his success?

3. What events destabilized Persia shortly before Alexander's invasion?

4. How did Alexander view Eastern cultures? What cultural changes did he encourage, and how did he do that?

5. What was Alexander's lasting legacy?

Chapter 9: The Hellenistic Age

"This is Alexander's ring!" General Perdiccas held the ring high. "He gave it to me on his deathbed. I shall rule as the regent for Arrhidaeus and Roxana's son."

The council of generals erupted in anger. "How do we know Roxana will have a son? Arrhidaeus isn't even fit to rule."

"He's Alexander's only living brother. Yes, he's not bright, but we can guide him," Perdiccas insisted. "If Roxana has a girl, Arrhidaeus will be our king. If she has a boy, we'll have two kings."

"And you'll have all the power," the generals complained.

"We will *all* have power," Perdiccas stated. "Each of you will rule a chunk of the empire."

The Partition of Babylon

What did the new leadership plan—the Partition of Babylon—look like? Perdiccas was to command the army and be the regent for Roxana's baby (if a son) and Arrhidaeus. The other generals, called the ***Diadochi*** (successors), each took a section of the empire. Antipater, Ptolemy, and Antigonus were the primary players. General Antipater continued to rule Greece and Macedonia. Alexander had appointed him as regent when he was away conquering the Persian Empire. Egypt went to General Ptolemy. One-eyed Antigonus got southwestern Turkey.

With that settled, Perdiccas walked through the palace to Roxana's room. "Time to tie up some loose ends."

Roxana nodded. "I have everything ready."

They swept into the room of Alexander's two Persian wives, Stateira and Parysatis II. Perdiccas nodded to the princesses. "The generals have made their decision. They will govern the provinces. I will be regent for Arrhidaeus and Roxana's child if it's a son."

Princess Parysatis frowned. "What happens to us?"

Roxana smiled reassuringly. "You can return to Persia or stay here in Babylon. Now, let's drink a toast to our departed husband and the future of his empire."

Perdiccas opened a new bottle and poured out four cups. He handed one to each woman and took a long drink from his cup. "May Alexander's legacy live on."

The three women drank from their cups. Then, Perdiccas and Roxana spoke a few more assuring words and left. As they walked down the corridor, Perdiccas turned to Roxana. "How?"

Roxana laughed. "The poison was in the cups, not the bottle. They'll be dead within hours."

Wars of the Diadochi

Roxana had a baby boy two months later. She named him Alexander IV. Arrhidaeus married his niece, Eurydice, in a match arranged by Perdiccas. Meanwhile, General Ptolemy stole Alexander's body when it was on its way to Macedonia for burial. He said, "Alexander wanted us to bury him in Egypt! I'm honoring his request." To this day, no one knows where Alexander's tomb is located.

In 322 BCE, Athenians rebelled against Antipater's rule over Greece in the Lamian War. They chased him out of southern Greece. Antipater

Seleucus I.[42]

would have lost the war if General Craterus of Macedonia hadn't come to the rescue. Together, they crushed the Athenian army in Thessaly. After this devastating loss, Antipater ended democracy in Athens. He forced the Athenians to submit to a council of elders.

Perdiccas didn't last long as regent. His officers rebelled and killed him. The generals worked out a new arrangement. Antipater became regent for Arrhidaeus and two-year-old Alexander IV. He brought them to Macedon. Seleucus, one of the officers involved in the plot against Perdiccas, became the ruler of Babylon. He eventually formed the Seleucid Empire, which covered the Middle East at its height.

Antipater died in 319 BCE. He appointed General Polyperchon as his replacement in his will. But Antipater's son, Cassander, refused to accept it. He allied with Ptolemy and Antigonus. They attacked Polyperchon. Polyperchon couldn't fend off three armies. He took Roxana and little Alexander to Epirus in northwest Greece, where he hoped they would be safe.

Olympias, Alexander the Great's mother.[43]

Alexander the Great's mother, Olympias, got involved in 317 BCE. Arrhidaeus was the son of her rival, one of Philip's other wives. She wanted her grandson, Alexander IV, to sit on the throne. She attacked Macedonia with General Polyperchon. The soldiers refused to fight Alexander the Great's mother. Olympias ordered Arrhidaeus's execution. Eurydice committed suicide.

The tables turned against Olympias when Ptolemy, Antigonus, and Cassander successfully attacked Macedon. Olympias was stoned to death. Polyperchon escaped to southern Greece. Cassander now ruled Macedonia and northern Greece. He locked Roxana and the boy-king Alexander in a tower for years. Eventually, he poisoned them. By that point, no one cared. The generals had become so powerful they were kings in their own right. Antigonus ruled Turkey, Lebanon, and Syria. Ptolemy was still the pharaoh of Egypt. Seleucus controlled much of the Middle East.

Showdown at Ipsus

In 302 BCE, southern Greece (except Sparta) united under Demetrius, the son of Antigonus. His enemy Cassander drummed up support in northern Greece. He also had the support of General Lysimachus in Thrace. Cassander invited Seleucus to join them in the war against Antigonus and Demetrius. Seleucus was wrapping up a war in north India. He lost, but he hashed out an agreeable settlement. King Chandragupta Maurya gave him five hundred war elephants. Seleucus gave Chandragupta his daughter to marry.

Seleucus marched to Turkey from India with his elephants. With Lysimachus marching in from Thrace, Antigonus desperately needed Demetrius to come help him. Demetrius blocked the Dardanelles when Cassander tried to send troops. Cassander then put his men on ships, but only one-third of the vessels made it. Demetrius captured some, and a storm sank the others. In the Battle of Ipsus, Antigonus and Demetrius had seventy thousand troops, ten thousand cavalry, and seventy-five elephants. The allies had sixty-four thousand foot soldiers, fifteen thousand cavalry, and Seleucus's five hundred elephants.

Seleucus launched a charge of two hundred elephants. Demetrius's seventy-five elephants were outnumbered. The main problem was that Demetrius's cavalry wasn't up to the challenge. The horses galloped off the field. However, Antigonus's foot soldiers began pushing the allied forces back.

Demetrius got his calvary under control, and the horses raced back on the field. It was time for Seleucus to bring out the rest of the elephants! The massive beasts frightened Demetrius's horses right back off the field. Seleucus brought his horses around on the other side, shattering Antigonus's phalanx. King Antigonus died in a hail of javelins. Demetrius ran off to Greece.

Hellenistic Culture Transforms Asia, Africa, and Europe

As the Greeks established cities in North Africa and Asia, they spread their philosophical, artistic, and scientific knowledge. The Greeks picked up aspects from the cultures of North Africa, the Middle East, and India. As Rome interacted with Greece, it imitated Greek sculptures, literature, and other cultural elements, spreading the Hellenistic culture throughout Europe.

Antioch in Syria and Alexandria in Egypt were two dynamic centers of Hellenism. Alexandria was the intellectual center. It had a mind-blowing library of a half million scrolls on history, literature, religion, and science. It had observatories for studying astronomy and laboratories for developing science. Mathematicians like Euclid and Eratosthenes taught there.

Alexander the Great and his successors spoke and wrote Koine Greek. It became the common language around the Mediterranean and in the Middle East.

Ptolemy II, Egypt's second Macedonian pharaoh."

Ptolemy II, Egypt's second Macedonian pharaoh, had the Jewish Tanakh (Old Testament) translated into Koine Greek. This Septuagint translation was used in Jewish synagogues in Jesus's day. The Apostles wrote the New Testament in Koine Greek.

What Happened to the Greek City-states?

Sparta's population was dwindling fast. Over two-thirds of its men died in battle. The fighting men had trouble maintaining their farms once the helots left. A few wealthy families held much of the land. Everyone else suffered under crushing debt. They had no way to feed their families. In 245 BCE, Agis IV became one of Sparta's kings. He had ideas for radical reform. He planned to forgive all debts and redivide all the farmland so every family had an equal plot again.

The wealthy landowners did not want to give up their land. They had the other king, Leonidas, on their side. When the council voted, Agis lost by one vote. But then Agis pulled out his trump card. "May I remind the council that Leonidas is more Persian than Spartan? He grew up in Persia and married a Persian woman, which is against our law. He lives a life of luxury rather than our simple Spartan ways."

It worked. The council kicked Leonidas out. Agis decided to hold off on land redistribution. That policy seemed too radical. However, he did cancel everyone's debts. But when he headed out to war, Leonidas snuck back into town and took his throne back. When Agis returned, Leonidas strangled him.

Cleomenes was Leonidas's son. One day, he returned from a hunting trip when his father announced he had arranged a marriage for him.

"To whom?"

"To Agiatis, the widow of Agis."

Cleomenes knew his father wanted the wealthy woman's estate. How on earth would this crazy marriage work? His father had killed her husband! Against all odds, the unlikely couple got along. Agiatis enthusiastically supported her first husband's reform plans. She convinced Cleomenes to follow through on them.

When Cleomenes became king, he introduced Agis's land redistribution plan. He started with his own land, which he handed it over to be divided up. His friends and family followed his lead. All the large landowners were eventually shamed into giving up their land. Sparta only had two thousand male citizens left, and the land was divided among them and the Perioikoi non-citizens.

Cleomenes's reforms were a good start, but Sparta's population was dropping at an alarming rate. The young men continued living in the barracks, so their wives didn't have many children. And then, in 222 BCE, it happened. Sparta suffered a horrifying loss against Macedonia in the Battle of Sellasia. Only two hundred of Sparta's men survived. Sparta was on the brink of extinction.

The Macedonian kingdom threatened to swallow up all of Greece's city-states. If they wanted to survive, they had two choices. The Greek cities could place themselves under another powerful Hellenistic kingdom, like Egypt or the Seleucid Empire. Option two was joining a Greek league and uniting with other Greek city-states. Athens took option one and allied with Egypt. It didn't work. Athens fell to

Macedonia in 261 BCE in the Chremonidean War.

The Aetolian League and the Achaean League were the two most powerful Greek leagues. The Aetolian League in central Greece successfully fought Macedonia. In 279 BCE, it protected Apollo's temple at Delphi from a Celtic invasion. Initially, the Aetolian League allied with the Roman Republic, but later, it fought with the Seleucid Empire against Rome.

The Achaean League was in the Peloponnese Peninsula, but Sparta never joined it. The league scored a thrilling victory by removing the Macedonians from the Peloponnese in 243 BCE. But then the league made the mistake of asking Macedonia for help fighting King Cleomenes of Sparta. They almost wiped the Spartans off the face of the earth, but the Macedonians were lording over them again. In the Second Macedonian War, the Achaean League joined forces with its former enemies, the Aetolian League. Success! They got rid of Macedonia's control.

King Pyrrhus of Epirus.[45]

Rome Emerges as a Superpower

Initially, the Roman Republic controlled only central Italy. In 280 BCE, it began to attack the wealthy Greek colonies in southern Italy. The Greeks asked King Pyrrhus of Epirus to help. Epirus was a poor city-state in northern Greece, but Pyrrhus had visions of grandeur. He dreamed of being another Alexander the Great. He rounded up ships and soldiers from his royal relatives in Egypt, Macedonia, and the Seleucid Empire. Then, he sailed to Italy.

Pyrrhus technically won his first battle against Rome. Still, he suffered such devastating losses that it was a **Pyrrhic victory**, which means it was not worth the win. His subsequent two battles were even worse. He went home, where he was killed by an old lady who threw a roof tile at him and knocked him off his horse.

Rome conquered the Greek city-states of Sicily in the First Punic War (264-241). While fighting Carthage and the Sicilian Greeks, Rome got involved in the Macedonian Wars. The Romans joined forces with the Aetolian League against Philip V of Macedonia. Sparta also jumped into the fray and allied with Rome and the Aetolian League. That didn't go well. The Peloponnese Greeks lost to Philip in 209 BCE.

However, in 198 BCE, Rome kicked Philip out of Greece. On Philip's way back to Macedonia, the Romans launched a surprise attack on his rear guard, killing two thousand of his men. Philip fought the Romans again in Thessaly the following year. An early morning fog covered the valley where the battle occurred. The Romans used war elephants for the first time in the Battle of Cynoscephalae. The Macedonians could hear them stomping and trumpeting. Then, the elephants suddenly appeared in the swirling mist. Philip lost eight thousand men that day. He had to give up his navy and army.

The Achaean League initially allied with Rome, but that relationship soured when Rome said the league couldn't expand its territory. The Achaean League revolted against Rome in 146 BCE. It lost most of its men in the Battle of Scarpheia near central Greece's eastern coast. Most of the survivors committed suicide. A few escaped to Corinth, but the Romans followed.

In less than a day, Rome defeated the Greeks at Corinth. Most of its citizens snuck out of the city, but the Romans killed any men who were left and enslaved the women and children. The Romans stripped

Corinth of its precious statues and artwork. They burned the ancient city to the ground. The rest of the Greek cities surrendered to Rome.

The Last Embers of the Hellenistic Kingdoms

What happened to the Hellenistic kingdoms? King Perseus of Macedon started the Third Macedonian War in 171 BCE. He made outlandish promises to get the Greek city-states to ally with him. When he conquered Thessaly, Rome sent troops to counter him. The Macedonians pounded the Romans into the dirt. They killed two thousand Romans and only lost four hundred of their own.

Perseus let the victory go to his head and let down his guard. Without warning, Rome's consul, Crassus, stormed in with his war elephants. Eight thousand Macedonians fell in one day. Perseus abandoned his army at Pydna, but the Romans tracked him down and dragged him to Rome. He spent the rest of his life in prison. After 168 BCE, Rome controlled Macedon. Macedon was divided into four provinces.

The Seleucid Empire was a dynamic hub of Hellenistic culture. At its height, it stretched from Syria to Afghanistan. However, the empire slowly declined after Seleucus's death. Persia's Parthian Empire eventually swallowed up the eastern part of the Seleucid Empire. The western part of the empire suffered civil wars and invasions until it fell under Roman control. General Pompey of Rome reorganized it into Roman provinces in 63 BCE.

Before the Seleucid Empire collapsed, its king triggered the Maccabean Revolt in Judea. In 167 BCE, Antiochus IV Epiphanes tried to force the Jews to mix the Greek religion with Judaism. When Jerusalem rebelled, he killed forty thousand Jews, including children and babies. He sacrificed a pig to Zeus in Jerusalem's temple. The enraged Jews fought against the Seleucid Greeks and kicked them out of Judea.

Egypt was a Macedonian kingdom for three centuries. Its pharaohs all came from Ptolemy. The Egyptian pharaohs married their sisters, and the Macedonian pharaohs did the same. Quarrels and power plays within the royal family weakened Egypt. Cleopatra was a co-pharaoh with her thirteen-year-old brother, Ptolemy XIII. She was also his wife. When Ptolemy got mad at Cleopatra and kicked her out, she started a steamy romance with a Roman named Julius Caesar. Caesar went to war against Egypt. Ptolemy XIII ended up drowning in the Nile.

Cleopatra, the Macedonian pharaoh of Egypt.[46]

Another of Cleopatra's brothers came to the throne. He was only twelve. It is believed he also married Cleopatra. However, she ran off with Caesar. She lived in his villa in Italy until the senators assassinated him in 44 BCE. Cleopatra then started a romance with a Roman consul, Mark Antony. Octavian was Antony's co-consul, and his sister, Octavia, was Antony's wife. He was furious when Antony abandoned his sister for Cleopatra. Octavian declared war against Egypt. Antony and Cleopatra lost the war. Both of them committed suicide, and Egypt became a Roman province.

Round-up Activity: Timeline

( ) Agis IV begins reforming Sparta.

( ) Antigonus dies in the Battle of Ipsus.

( ) Athens falls to Macedonia in the Chremonidean War.

( ) Maccabean Revolt begins. The Jews kick the Greeks out of Judea.

( ) Olympias orders Arrhidaeus's execution.

( ) Partition of Babylon.

( ) Peloponnese Greeks lose to Philip V of Macedonia.

( ) Rome attacks Greek colonies in southern Italy.

( ) Rome burns Corinth to the ground and steals priceless art.

( ) Roxana has a baby boy, Alexander IV.

Chapter 10: Greek Science and Technology

The ancient Greeks changed the world. They gave rise to awe-inspiring breakthroughs in science and technology. As the Greek culture spread to Egypt and the Middle East, it created an exciting exchange of ideas. People became even more interested in science, math, and medicine. This intellectual growth took the world by storm.

Pythagoras

Pythagoras was a math genius who lived in the 6th century BCE. He grew up on the island of Samos. As a young adult, Pythagoras lived as a hermit in a cave. He did not eat meat. Pythagoras later moved to southern Italy and set up a school. His students were also vegetarians and lived a simple life. It was similar to a commune. Everyone shared everything.

Most people back then thought the world was flat. Pythagoras challenged this idea. He taught that it was a sphere, like a ball. He might have been the first to introduce this groundbreaking idea. Pythagoras was the first in the Greek world to develop the *Pythagorean theorem*, although the Babylonians used it centuries earlier.

What is the Pythagorean theorem? It starts with a triangle with a right angle (a ninety-degree angle). Opposite the right angle is the longest side of the triangle: the hypotenuse. If you square each of the two shorter sides, it equals the hypotenuse squared.

$$a^2 + b^2 = c^2$$

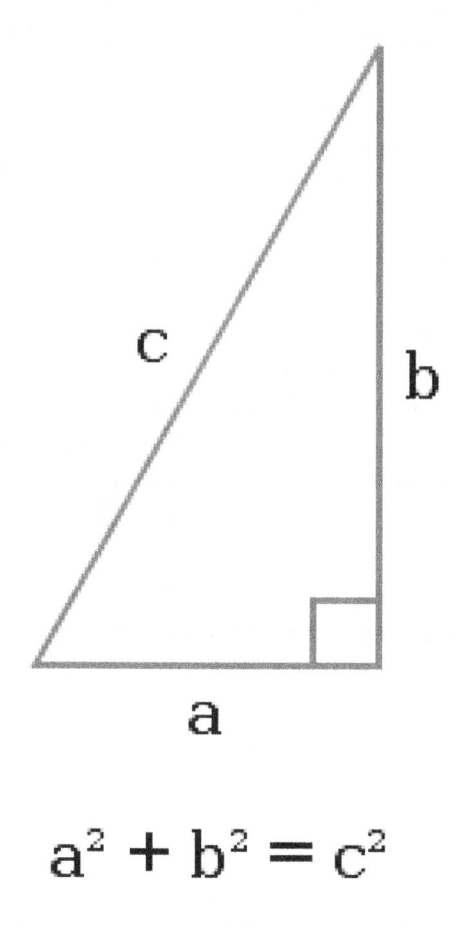

In this right triangle, "c" is the hypotenuse or longest side.[47]

Hippocrates, the Father of Modern Medicine

Our medical legacy owes an outstanding debt to Hippocrates. He lived in the 5th century BCE and learned medicine from his father and grandfather. Plato said he was an "Asclepiad," or a healing priest. In his day and age, people thought sickness was a curse from the gods. Hippocrates taught a revolutionary new idea. He said that diseases had natural causes. He suggested that what a person ate, how they lived, and their environment affected their health.

Hippocrates was the first to use *clinical diagnosis*. This included things that are a normal part of doctor visits today, like checking a person's pulse and temperature. He observed a person's range of motion and asked about their urine and bowel movements. He used all this information when making a diagnosis. He thought the body could heal itself and that the doctor's job was to help this process. For some health problems, he recommended fasting for a short time. He also used a mixture of honey and vinegar for some illnesses.

Hippocrates, Father of Modern Medicine.[48]

New doctors still quote the Hippocratic Oath, although the words have changed over the centuries. The original oath included some of the following promises:

1. I will soothe the pain of anyone who needs my art, and if I don't know how, I will seek the counsel of my teachers.
2. I will never harm my suffering friend because life is sacred.
3. I pray that the attention I give to those who put themselves in my hands is rewarded with happiness.
4. I swear to care for anyone who suffers, prince or slave.

Leucippus and Democritus Develop Atomic Theory

Leucippus and his student Democritus lived in the 5th century BCE. These brilliant ancient scientists developed the early principles of atoms and nuclear physics. What did they have to say about atoms?

1. The universe is made of "Being" (the physical world or matter) and "Void" (empty space).
2. Atoms are countless super-tiny particles that can't be changed or divided.

3. These atoms constantly move and form everything in the physical world.
4. Groups of atoms can change into various arrangements, making distinct types of matter.

Democritus was also interested in genetics. He wrote a letter to Hippocrates, saying that a man and woman both make "seeds." These seeds contain information about every part of the body. They come together to form a new body.

Architectural Wonders

Polycrates was the tyrant of Samos when Pythagoras lived there. Remember, tyrants were not necessarily evil. They often improved the lives of people. For instance, Polycrates built a *mole*. This was like a causeway sticking out into the sea. A mole kept waves and strong currents from destroying the harbor.

What really made Polycrates famous was the Tunnel of Eupalinos. The tunnel was named after its engineer. It was a half-mile (one-kilometer) aqueduct that went straight through a mountain! Two teams carved the tunnel. They began on opposite sides of the mountain and met in the middle. The Greek historian Herodotus said this was one of the most extraordinary feats in the Greek world.

Ictinus was an architect who pulled off another engineering triumph in the 5th century BCE. He built the lovely Parthenon temple in Athens. It had elegant Doric columns. It was a breathtaking showcase of balance and had intricate details. Ictinus put *entasis* into play. He put slight bulges in the columns to create an optical illusion of perfectly straight pillars.

The Parthenon.[49]

Giant amphitheaters were also popular in ancient Greece. Even before the Dark Ages, the Greeks built semi-circular outdoor theaters for dramatic performances. How did people hear the actors in the days before microphones? Well, the architects used incredible acoustic engineering technology. Modern scientists tested it on the ancient theater ruins at Epidaurus, near Athens. Even today, if one drops a coin, it can be heard throughout the theater.

By the 3rd century, these arenas had become huge. The one in Ephesus could seat twenty-four thousand people! Greek architects built theaters where there was a beautiful view, such as on a mountain or overlooking the sea. If people got bored with the show, they could enjoy the view!

Theaetetus of Athens

Theaetetus was a 4th-century BCE mathematician. He was a student of Socrates. He made giant leaps in the field of geometry. Theaetetus figured out that there could only be five ***Platonic solids***. A Platonic solid has "faces" that are ***polygons***, flat shapes with straight edges. Only three polygons can make a Platonic solid: squares, triangles, and pentagons (a shape with five sides). In a Platonic solid, all the faces have to be identical. The same number of polygons meet at each corner of the shape.

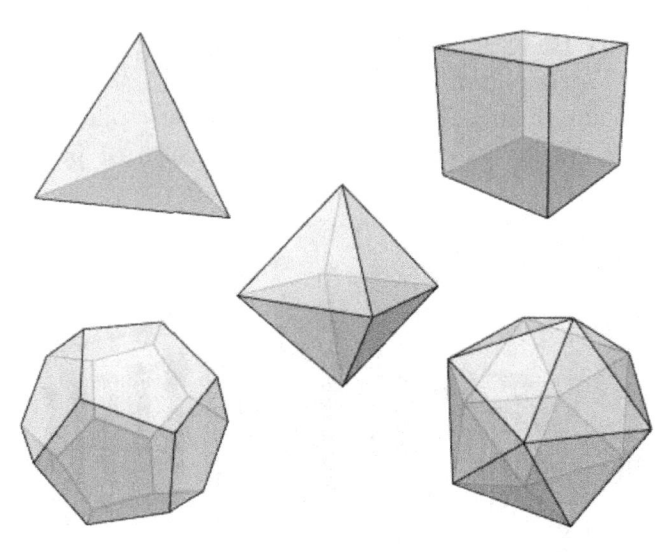

The five Platonic solids are the tetrahedron (or pyramid), cube, octahedron (eight faces), dodecahedron (twelve faces), and icosahedron (twenty faces).[50]

Theaetetus explored *irrational lengths*. What are those? The Greeks believed that numbers measured the length of something. Irrational numbers are numbers that aren't rational. They have no repeating pattern and cannot be fractions. Irrational numbers aren't usual numbers like one, four, seven, or nine. They are numbers like pi (π), which starts with 3.14159.

Euclid of Alexandria

Euclid was a 4th-century BCE mathematician who wrote the *Elements*, a collection of thirteen textbooks on math and geometry. His book was a collection of earlier mathematicians' work. Euclid developed their work further. For instance, he tweaked Theaetetus's theorems so they were more accurate. Euclid provided solid proof of the theories of earlier mathematicians. He ran a school in Alexandria, Egypt, in the early 300s when it was a new city.

Aristarchus of Samos

Aristarchus was a 3rd-century BCE astronomer. He was the first to say that the earth rotates on its axis once a day. Aristarchus said the sun was at the center of the universe. He believed the earth revolved around the sun once a year, along with the other planets. He also thought the stars were suns that were far, far away. Most people thought Aristarchus was a bit crazy thinking these kinds of things. They believed the earth was the center of the universe. It took eighteen centuries before Nicolaus Copernicus's model of the universe with the sun at its center caught on.

Archimedes of Syracuse

Archimedes was a 3rd-century BCE mathematician, scientist, and inventor. He founded *theoretical mechanics* (how things move under the action of force). Archimedes developed the *law of the lever*. Think about a see-saw. If the person on one end weighs twice as much as the person on the other, the smaller person would be stuck in the air. But what if the heavier person moves toward the center (*fulcrum*) of the see-saw? Then, they would both be balanced. We can use this principle to move heavy objects with a long stick and a big rock. Archimedes supposedly said, "Give me a place to stand, and I shall move the earth!"

Law of the lever.[51]

Archimedes built on the lever concept and made the first ***compound pulley***. A compound pulley consists of a fixed pulley that doesn't move and a moveable second pulley attached to the load. The combination of pulleys gives greater lifting ability because the weight is distributed. It also allows more flexibility when changing directions. He demonstrated this tool's power by moving a ship all by himself!

Archimedes also discovered that if you place a solid in a fluid, it is lighter than the fluid it displaces. For instance, let's say you're a bigger person. You go swimming, and you notice that you can easily float despite your weight. In fact, you find it easier to float than your thin friend. Why? The buoyant force pushes you up. The water is denser than your body is, especially if you have a lot of body fat. That's why ships can float. Rocks can't float, though; they're denser than water.

Archimedes didn't stop with levers, compound pulleys, and floating heavy objects. He worked out a formula for the volume of a ***sphere*** (a ball shape). He also discovered the ratio of the distance around a circle (its ***circumference***) compared to its ***diameter*** (a line going through the circle's middle). He called this the "ratio of circumference to diameter pi" (π) and calculated it to be 3.14159.

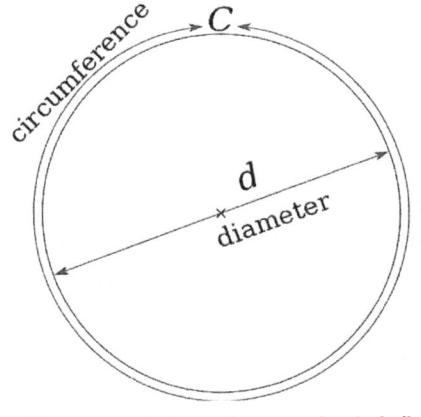

Diameter and circumference of a circle.[52]

Eratosthenes of Alexandria

The bustling city of Alexandria on Egypt's Mediterranean coast had a priceless library of books on science, math, history, religion, and literature. In the 2nd century BCE, its head librarian was Eratosthenes. By his time, Greeks had gradually accepted that the earth was not flat but a sphere. "How big is the earth?" Eratosthenes wondered. And this is where things get wild—he figured it out!

As a librarian, Eratosthenes tended to read a lot. One day, he read something interesting about the nearby city of Syene (Aswan, Egypt). On the summer solstice (June 21st), the sun lit up the bottom of a well at noon. This meant the sun was directly overhead. "I wonder if the same thing happens in Alexandria?" he mused.

So, Eratosthenes went outside on the summer solstice at noon and plunged a stick into the ground. It cast a slight shadow that had an angle of about seven degrees. Syene was fifty miles (eighty kilometers) from Alexandria. "If the sun casts a shadow here at noon but not in Syene, it's because the earth is curved," he decided. "Seven degrees is about 1/50th the circumference of a complete circle."

Using his knowledge of geometry, Eratosthenes worked out some figures. He decided that the distance around the earth was about twenty-eight thousand miles (forty-five thousand kilometers). He was really close! Calculations today place the earth's circumference at 24,901 miles.

What a mind-blowing legacy the ancient Greeks left us! These sharp-witted people discovered things that we take for granted. The knowledge they accumulated and built on is almost overwhelming to think about. We owe so much to them in the fields of philosophy, medicine, mathematics, science, and astronomy. The accomplishments of the ancient Greeks stretch through time to touch our lives today.

Round-up Activity: One-pager

In this activity, you will create your own Greek history page focusing on science and technology in ancient Greece. It can be a normal-sized page, like the size of copy paper, or you can make a poster. Use pictures to illustrate important people or their contributions. Draw your own or print photos off the internet. Describe key players and how they advanced science, math, or technology. You may want to include a timeline. You can choose to cover one unit of time, such as the Classical period or the Hellenistic Age. Or you could focus on a specific field, such as geometry, medicine, or architecture. Get creative with your favorite colors (or colors that symbolize Greece). Don't forget to make an eye-catching border.

Use your imagination and have fun!

Answer Key for Round-up Activities

Chapter 1: Timeline Game

(2) A catastrophic volcanic eruption wipes out all life on the island of Thera.

(7) A horrible plague kills one-third of Athens's population.

(10) Battle of Corinth: Rome conquered the Greek Achaean League.

(5) Cleisthenes brings democratic reform to Athens.

(4) First Olympic Games.

(3) The Greek Dark Ages.

(1) Minoans develop Greece's first writing system, Linear A.

(8) The Greek League of Corinth forms to invade the Persian Empire under Alexander.

(6) The Greeks unite to crush the Persian fleet in the naval Battle of Mycale.

(9) When Alexander the Great dies, his generals fight for control in the Wars of the Diadochi.

Chapter 2: Who's Who?

1. Aphrodite
2. Apollo
3. Ares
4. Artemis
5. Athena
6. Demeter
7. Dionysus
8. Hephaistos
9. Hera
10. Hermes
11. Poseidon
12. Zeus

A. King of the gods and of rain

B. Queen of the gods and vengeful wife of Zeus

C. Goddess of love and mother of Aeneas

D. The disabled god of crafts and volcanoes

E. God of the sun, music, archery, and healing

F. God of war and one of Aphrodite's lovers

G. Goddess of nature, wild animals, and hunting

H. Goddess of wisdom who split open Zeus's head

I. Goddess of farmers and the earth's fertility

J. The messenger god with winged sandals

K. God of the seas and father of the Cyclopes

L. God of wine, insanity, theater, and festivals

Chapter 3: Word Search

E	S	P	A	L	L	O	C	E	G	A	E	Z	N	O	R	B
T	I		I	N	F	R	A	S	T	R	U	C	T	U	R	E
A	E		C	A			N	Y	M	A	G	Y	L	O	P	
T	R		E	I				A								
S	A		A	N				R								
Y	N		R	O			Y			C						
T	E		G	C		R				H						
I	C		A	A	W			T	N	A	R	Y	T			
C	R		N	R	O											
	E		G	D												
			M	A												
				M												

1. The sudden fall of multiple civilizations in the eastern Mediterranean around 1200 BCE (Bronze Age collapse)
2. Marriage to more than one person (polygamy)
3. One large independent city ruling over towns and villages in the surrounding area (city-state)
4. "Great Greece" region of southern Italy (Magna Graecia)
5. An absolute ruler who came to power outside the usual channels (tyrant)

6. Something that is inhumane or unusually cruel (draconian)
7. Money or property a bride brings into a marriage (dowry)
8. Disorder because of governmental breakdown (anarchy)
9. Public works like roads, bridges, and sewers (infrastructure)
10. Soldiers who are paid to fight for another city-state or country (mercenaries)

Chapter 4: Review Questions

1. How did Sparta's culture and society differ from other ancient Greek city-states?
    - ➤ It had a different political system with two kings.
    - ➤ Boys were educated away from home from age seven.
    - ➤ Women had more rights.
    - ➤ The helot system provided labor. Spartan men did not work their own farms.
2. What role did military service play in Spartan society?
    - ➤ All Spartan men under age sixty were full-time soldiers.
    - ➤ Boys trained for military life from the age of seven.
    - ➤ Young married men lived in barracks rather than with their wives.
3. What was the agoge? How did it shape the upbringing and education of Spartan boys?
    - ➤ The agoge was the military training and educational system for boys from age seven to thirty.
    - ➤ It taught the boys discipline, endurance, simplicity, patriotism, and military skills.
4. What challenges did Spartan boys face in their rigorous training and education?
    - ➤ They endured harsh treatment, like sleeping outside and hazing.
    - ➤ They often did not have enough food.
5. What were some positive aspects of Sparta's legacy?
    - ➤ The culture promoted self-discipline, self-sacrifice, and courage.

> Women had an elevated status (compared to other Greek women) in Spartan society.
6. How has Sparta's legacy negatively impacted some civilizations?
   > It influenced the state control of families
   > The goal of military conquest was more important than a healthy family life.
   > They practiced infanticide and ethnic cleansing (killing the helots).

Chapter 5: Fill in the Blank

The Persian Wars with Greece began when Cyrus the Great conquered _Ionia__ in 547 BCE, making these Greek colonies a province of the Persian-Achaemenid Empire. When Ionia revolted in 499 BCE, Athens and _Eretria_ sent ships and troops to help. After ending the revolt, the Persian king, Darius the Great, sent his fleet to punish Athens. However, the Athenians chose the battleground in a marshy area where the Persians couldn't use their horses. They soundly defeated the Persians in the _Battle of Marathon_, where the marshy terrain kept the Persians from using their horses. Xerxes, the son of Darius, sought revenge and marched into Greece with a huge army. Led by the Spartan king _Leonidas_, the Greeks held off the Persians at the __Thermopylae Pass_ while the rest of the Greeks evacuated _Athens_ and rebuilt the wall at the _Isthmus of Corinth_. The Greeks sacrificed themselves at the pass, but in the end, the Greeks scored an astounding victory in the naval _Battle of Salamis_.

Chapter 7: True or False?

1. Homer gave an eyewitness account of the Peloponnesian War. (It was Thucydides) **(F)**
2. The Athenians resettled the helots at Naupaktos. **(T)**
3. Athens also fought in North Africa during the first war. **(T)**
4. Thucydides thought going to war was a great idea. (He warned them to count the cost) **(F)**

5. The plague didn't kill many people in Athens. (It killed one-third of the population) **(F)**
6. The fifty-year Peace of Nicias only lasted six years. **(T)**
7. The war moved to Sicily when Athens agreed to help Segesta. **(T)**
8. General Nicias made quick and sound decisions that won the war in Sicily. (He constantly delayed and made mostly poor decisions) **(F)**
9. Alcibiades switched sides to Sparta and then back to Athens again. **(T)**
10. Athens won the final Battle of Aegospotami against Sparta. (Sparta crushed them, ending the war) **(F)**

Chapter 8: Quiz

1. In what ways did Alexander's upbringing and education influence his leadership style and approach to conquest?
    - Aristotle taught him ethics, politics, and logic, which shaped his leadership skills. He learned military strategies from reading the *Iliad*. He also learned Classical Greek culture, enabling him to communicate effectively with his Greek forces.
    - His father, Philip II, taught him military arts and provided him with opportunities to put them into practice.
2. What were some of the key military tactics that Alexander the Great used in his conquests? How did these tactics contribute to his success?
    - He used the element of surprise.
    - He used a blend of skills and tools: a new phalanx position, the sarissas, cavalry, and ingenious siege technology.
    - He tended to use the same line-up for his battles. His soldiers always knew what to do.
    - He made effective decisions on the spur of the moment.
3. What events destabilized Persia shortly before Alexander's invasion?
    - Most of the Persian royal males were poisoned.
    - Darius III was abruptly brought to the throne with little preparation to rule an empire.

4. How did Alexander view Eastern cultures? What cultural changes did he encourage, and how did he do that?
    - He admired Eastern culture, adopted some customs, and planned to restore Babylon.
    - Eastern and Western cultures were fused. For instance, Greek officers married Persian princesses.
    - He built over two dozen cities named Alexandria that promoted Hellenistic culture.
5. What was Alexander's lasting legacy?
    - He developed military strategies that are still studied today.
    - He developed a cultural fusion of Eastern and Western cultures.
    - He spread the Greek Hellenistic culture to Asia and North Africa.

Chapter 9: Timeline

(7) Agis IV begins reforming Sparta. (245)

(4) Antigonus dies in the Battle of Ipsus. (302)

(6) Athens falls to Macedonia in the Chremonidean War. (261)

(9) Maccabean Revolt begins. The Jews kick the Greeks out of Judea. (167)

(3) Olympias orders Arrhidaeus's execution. (317)

(1) Partition of Babylon. (323)

(8) Peloponnese Greeks lose to Philip V of Macedonia. (209)

(5) Rome attacks Greek colonies in southern Italy. (280)

(10) Rome burns Corinth to the ground and steals priceless art. (146)

(2) Roxana has a baby boy, Alexander IV. (323)

If you enjoyed this book, a review on Amazon would be greatly appreciated because it would mean a lot to hear from you.

To leave a review:
1. Open your camera app.
2. Point your mobile device at the QR code.
3. The review page will appear in your web browser.

Thanks for your support!

Here's another book by Enthralling History that you might like

Free limited time bonus

We forget 90% of everything that we've read in 7 days...

Get the free printable pdf summary of the book you've read AND much, much more... shhhh...

Enter Your Most Frequently Used Email to Get Started

DOWNLOAD FREE PDF SUMMARY

© Enthralling History

Stop for a moment. We have a free bonus set up for you. The problem is this: we forget 90% of everything that we read after 7 days. Crazy fact, right? Here's the solution: we've created a printable, 1-page pdf summary for this book that you're reading now. All you have to do to get your free pdf summary is to go to the following website: https://livetolearn.lpages.co/enthrallinghistory/

Or, Scan the QR code!

Once you do, it will be intuitive. Enjoy, and thank you!

Bibliography

Arrian. "Alexander the Great." In *The Anabasis and the Indica.* Translated by Martin Hammond. Oxford: Oxford University Press, 2013.

Austin, M. M. "Greek Tyrants and the Persians, 546-479 B. C." *The Classical Quarterly* 40, no. 2 (1990): 289-306. http://www.jstor.org/stable/639090.

Bennett, Bob, and Mike Roberts. *The Wars of Alexander's Successors, 323-281 BC (Commanders and Campaigns Book 1).* South Yorkshire: Pen & Sword Military, 2013.

Bennett, Bob, and Mike Roberts. *The Wars of Alexander's Successors 323 - 281 BC. Volume 2: Battles and Tactics.* South Yorkshire: Pen & Sword Military, 2009.

Cartledge, Paul. *The Spartans: The World of the Warrior-Heroes of Ancient Greece.* New York: The Overlook Press, 2003.

Clogg, Richard. *A Concise History of Greece.* Cambridge: Cambridge University Press, 2021.

Guthrie, W. K. C. *A History of Greek Philosophy.* Cambridge: Cambridge University Press, 1979.

Guthrie, W. K. C. *The Sophists.* Cambridge: Cambridge University Press, 1977.

Herodotus, *The Histories.* Translated by George Rawlinson. New York: Dutton & Co, 1862. http://classics.mit.edu/Herodotus/history.html

Hippocrates' Oath. Translated by Amelia Arenas. Boston University. https://www.bu.edu/arion/files/2010/03/Arenas_05Feb2010_Layout-3.pdf

Homer. *The Iliad.* Translated by Samuel Butler. Internet Classics Archive. http://classics.mit.edu/Homer/iliad.html

Homer. *The Odyssey*. Translated by Samuel Butler. Internet Classics Archive.
http://classics.mit.edu/Homer/odyssey.html

Isocrates. *Letters*. Perseus Digital Library. Tufts University.
http://www.perseus.tufts.edu/hopper/text?doc=Perseus:text:1999.01.0246:letter=3.

Martin, Thomas R. *Ancient Greece: From Prehistoric to Hellenistic Times*. New Haven: Yale University Press, 1996.

Matyszak, Philip. *Greece Against Rome: The Fall of the Hellenistic Kingdoms 250-31 BC*. South Yorkshire: Pen & Sword Military, 2020.

Matyszak, Philip. *The Rise of the Hellenistic Kingdoms, 336-250 BC*. South Yorkshire: Pen & Sword Military, 2019.

Napoli, Donna Jo. *Treasury of Greek Mythology: Classic Stories of Gods, Goddesses, Heroes & Monsters*. Washington, D.C.: National Geographic Kids, 2011.

Nur, A., & E. H. Cline. "Poseidon's Horses: Plate Tectonics and Earthquake Storms in the Late Bronze Age Aegean and Eastern Mediterranean." *Journal of Archaeological Science*, 27(1), (2000): 43-63.
https://doi.org/10.1006/jasc.1999.0431

Plato. *The Republic*. Translated by Benjamin Jowett. Internet Classics Archive.
http://classics.mit.edu/Plato/republic.9.viii.html

Polybius. *Histories*.
http://www.perseus.tufts.edu/hopper/text?doc=Perseus:text:1999.01.0234

Plutarch. *Cimon*. Translated by John Dryden. Internet Classics Archive.
http://classics.mit.edu/Plutarch/cimon.html

Pomeroy, Sarah B., Stanley M. Burstein, Walter Donlan, Jennifer Tolbert Roberts, David W. Tandy, and Georgia Tsouvala. *Ancient Greece: Politics, Society, and Culture*. New York: Oxford University Press, 2020.

Rhodes, P. J. *Athenian Democracy* (Edinburgh Readings on the Ancient World). Oxford: Oxford University Press, 2004.

Rodgers, Nigel. *Ancient Greece: An Illustrated History: The Illustrated Encyclopedia; A Comprehensive History With 1000 Images*. Dayton, Ohio: Lorenz Books, 2017.

Stein, Daniel. "Plague, Climate Change, and the End of Ancient Civilizations." *Discentes*. June 25:2023.
https://web.sas.upenn.edu/discentes/2023/06/25/plague-climate-change-and-the-end-of-ancient-civilizations/

Thucydides. *History of the Peloponnesian War*. Translated by Rex Warner. New York: Penguin Classics, 1972.

Worthington, Ian. *By the Spear: Philip II, Alexander the Great, and the Rise and Fall of the Macedonian Empire (Ancient Warfare and Civilization)*. Oxford: Oxford University Press, 2016.

Xenophon. *The Landmark Xenophon's Hellenika*. Translated by John Marincola. New York: Anchor, 2010.

Image Sources

[1] Roman Eisele, CC BY-SA 4.0 <https://creativecommons.org/licenses/by-sa/4.0>, via Wikimedia Commons; https://commons.wikimedia.org/wiki/File:Mundelsheim_-_M%C3%BChlbachweinberge_-_Weinbergmauern_beim_Steinbruch_(1).jpg

[2] Photo Modified: labels added. Source: Peterfitzgerald (Peter Fitzgerald), Shaundd, CC BY-SA 4.0 <https://creativecommons.org/licenses/by-sa/4.0>, via Wikimedia Commons: https://commons.wikimedia.org/wiki/File:Greece_WV_regions_map_2016.svg

[3] RickyBennison, CC0, via Wikimedia Commons; https://commons.wikimedia.org/wiki/File:Panathenaic_Amphora_Sprinters.jpg

[4] https://commons.wikimedia.org/wiki/File:A_muse_with_a_harp,_and_two_others_with_Lyres_from_a_Greek_vase_in_the_Munich_Museum.jpg

[5] William Neuheisel from DC, US, CC BY 2.0 <https://creativecommons.org/licenses/by/2.0>, via Wikimedia Commons; https://commons.wikimedia.org/wiki/File:Lions_Gate_at_Mycenae_(5228010382).jpg

[6] Zde, CC BY-SA 4.0 <https://creativecommons.org/licenses/by-sa/4.0>, via Wikimedia Commons: https://commons.wikimedia.org/wiki/File:Middle_Corinthian_pottery_amphora,_Geledakis_Painter,_590-570_BC,_AM_Corinth,_Korm421.jpg

[7] Yair Haklai, CC BY-SA 3.0 <https://creativecommons.org/licenses/by-sa/3.0>, via Wikimedia Commons; https://commons.wikimedia.org/wiki/File:Antonio_Canova-Helen_of_Troy-Victoria_and_Albert_Museum.jpg

[8] Photo zoomed in. Source: Ricardo André Frantz (User:Tetraktys), CC BY-SA 3.0 <https://creativecommons.org/licenses/by-sa/3.0>, via Wikimedia Commons: https://commons.wikimedia.org/wiki/File:Netuno16b.jpg

[9] ArchaiOptix, CC BY-SA 4.0 <https://creativecommons.org/licenses/by-sa/4.0>, via Wikimedia Commons: https://commons.wikimedia.org/wiki/File:Group_of_Polygnotos_ARV_1057_98_return_of_Hephaistos_-_three_maenads_(0.5).jpg

[10] https://commons.wikimedia.org/wiki/File:Mattei_Athena_Louvre_Ma530_n2.jpg

[11] Zde, CC BY-SA 4.0 <https://creativecommons.org/licenses/by-sa/4.0>, via Wikimedia Commons: https://commons.wikimedia.org/wiki/File:Oracle_of_Delphi,_red-figure_kylix,_440-430_BC,_Kodros_Painter,_Berlin_F_2538,_141668.jpg

[12] Mary Harrsch, CC BY-SA 4.0 <https://creativecommons.org/licenses/by-sa/4.0>, via Wikimedia Commons: https://commons.wikimedia.org/wiki/File:Menelaus_bearing_the_corpse_of_Patroclus,_Marble,_Flavian_Era_(1st_century_CE)_Roman_copy_after_a_Hellenistic_original_of_the_3rd_century_BCE_MH_04.jpg

[13] Photo Modified: zoomed in, labels added. Source: Peripheries_of_Greece_numbered.svg: *Greek_Macedonia_map_with_subdivisions.svg: *Greece_2011_Periferiakes_Enotites.svg: Pitichinaccioderivative work: Philly boy92 (talk)derivative work: Fulvio314, CC BY-SA 3.0 <https://creativecommons.org/licenses/by-sa/3.0>, via Wikimedia Commons: https://commons.wikimedia.org/wiki/File:Greece_(ancient)_Epirus.svg

[14] Photo zoomed in. Source: George E. Koronaios, CC0, via Wikimedia Commons; https://commons.wikimedia.org/wiki/File:The_Temple_of_Athena_Nike_on_the_Acropolis_of_Athens_on_13_February_2019.jpg

[15] https://commons.wikimedia.org/wiki/File:Solon.jpg

[16] https://commons.wikimedia.org/wiki/File:Return_of_Peisistratus_to_Athens_with_the_false_Minerva.jpg

[17] Mary Harrsch, CC BY-SA 4.0 <https://creativecommons.org/licenses/by-sa/4.0>, via Wikimedia Commons: https://commons.wikimedia.org/wiki/File:Bronze_banqueter_from_the_tripod_support_of_a_bronze_bowl_Laconian_530-500_BCE_from_Dodona_British_Museum.jpg

[18] user:Megistias background cleaned by Chabacano, CC BY-SA 3.0 <http://creativecommons.org/licenses/by-sa/3.0/>, via Wikimedia Commons: https://commons.wikimedia.org/wiki/File:Hoplites.jpg

[19] Caeciliusinhorto, CC BY-SA 4.0 <https://creativecommons.org/licenses/by-sa/4.0>, via Wikimedia Commons; https://commons.wikimedia.org/wiki/File:Spartan_running_girl_(cropped).jpg

[20] Mary Harrsch, CC BY-SA 4.0 <https://creativecommons.org/licenses/by-sa/4.0>, via Wikimedia Commons: https://commons.wikimedia.org/wiki/File:Statue_of_a_hoplite_known_as_Leonidas_480-470_BCE_Sparta_Acropolis_Sanctuary_of_Athena_Chalkioikos_01.jpg

[21] https://commons.wikimedia.org/wiki/File:Greek_Galleys.jpg

[22] https://commons.wikimedia.org/wiki/File:The_Battle_of_Marathon.jpg

[23] https://commons.wikimedia.org/wiki/File:Construction_of_Xerxes_Bridge_of_boats_by_Phoenician_sailors.jpg

[24] *Photo modified: zoomed in, labels added. Source: Greece_location_map.svg: Lencer / derivative work: Uwe Dedering, CC BY-SA 3.0 <https://creativecommons.org/licenses/by-sa/3.0>, via Wikimedia Commons: https://commons.wikimedia.org/wiki/File:Greece_relief_location_map.jpg*

[25] https://commons.wikimedia.org/wiki/File:Ship_dashed_against_ship,_till_the_Persian_Army_dead_strewed_the_deep_like_flowers.jpg

[26] *lensnmatter, CC BY 2.0 https://creativecommons.org/licenses/by/2.0>, via Wikimedia Commons: https://commons.wikimedia.org/wiki/File:Caryatids_of_Erechtheion_(204196584.95).jpg*

[27] *Metropolitan Museum of Art, CC0, via Wikimedia Commons: https://commons.wikimedia.org/wiki/File:Terracotta_Nolan_amphora_(jar)_MET_DT229457.jpg*

[28] *Photo zoomed in. Source: ArchaiOptix, CC BY-SA 4.0 <https://creativecommons.org/licenses/by-sa/4.0>, via Wikimedia Commons: https://commons.wikimedia.org/wiki/File:Attic_red_figure_kylix_-_ARV_extra_-_symposion_-_Athens_NAM_1357.jpg*

[29] *ArchaiOptix, CC BY-SA 4.0 <https://creativecommons.org/licenses/by-sa/4.0>, via Wikimedia Commons: https://commons.wikimedia.org/wiki/File:Very_early_red_figure_pot_ARV_11_1_Dionysos_with_maenads_-_Achilles_and_Ajax_playing_(06).jpg*

[30] *Photograph by Dean Dixon, Sculpture by Alan LeQuire, FAL, via Wikimedia Commons: https://commons.wikimedia.org/wiki/File:Athena_Parthenos_LeQuire.jpg*

[31] *Photo zoomed in. Source: Jacques-Louis David, CC0, via Wikimedia Commons: https://commons.wikimedia.org/wiki/File:The_Death_of_Socrates_MET_DT40.jpg*

[32] *Vatican Museums, CC BY 3.0 <https://creativecommons.org/licenses/by/3.0>, via Wikimedia Commons: https://commons.wikimedia.org/wiki/File:Pericles_Pio-Clementino_Inv269_n4.jpg*

[33] *Photo Modified: zoomed in, labels added.* https://commons.wikimedia.org/wiki/File:Pineios_river_(Peloponnese).jpg

[34] *Yair Haklai, CC BY-SA 4.0 <https://creativecommons.org/licenses/by-sa/4.0>, via Wikimedia Commons: https://commons.wikimedia.org/wiki/File:Thucydides_at_Exterior_of_the_Austrian_Parliament_Building.jpg*

[35] *Photo zoomed in. Source: Morn, CC BY-SA 4.0 <https://creativecommons.org/licenses/by-sa/4.0>, via Wikimedia Commons: https://commons.wikimedia.org/wiki/File:Sicilian_Expedition_map_en.svg*

[36] https://commons.wikimedia.org/wiki/File:Bust_Alcibiades_Musei_Capitolini_MC1160_(cropped).jpg

[37] *Jona Lendering, CC0, via Wikimedia Commons:* https://commons.wikimedia.org/wiki/File:Philip_II_statue_350-400_CE.jpg

[38] *Photo modified: zoomed in and labels added. Source: ArnoldPlaton, CC BY-SA 3.0 <https://creativecommons.org/licenses/by-sa/3.0>, via Wikimedia Common:* https://commons.wikimedia.org/wiki/File:Balkan_Peninsula.svg

[39] https://commons.wikimedia.org/wiki/File:Alexander_The_Great_statue_-_estatua_de_Alejandro_Magno.jpg

[40] https://commons.wikimedia.org/wiki/File:Meister_der_Alexanderschlacht_003.jpg

[41] https://commons.wikimedia.org/wiki/File:The_charge_of_the_Persian_scythed_chariots_at_the_battle_of_Gaugamela_by_Andre_Castaigne_(1898-1899).jpg

[42] *Massimo Finizio, CC BY-SA 2.0 via Wikimedia Commons:* https://commons.wikimedia.org/wiki/File:Seleuco_I_Nicatore.JPG

[43] *Fotogeniss, CC BY-SA 3.0 <https://creativecommons.org/licenses/by-sa/3.0>, via Wikimedia Commons:* https://commons.wikimedia.org/wiki/File:Coin_olympias_mus_theski.JPG

[44] *Naples National Archaeological Museum, CC BY 2.5 <https://creativecommons.org/licenses/by/2.5>, via Wikimedia Commons:* https://commons.wikimedia.org/wiki/File:Ptolemy_II_MAN_Napoli_Inv5600.jpg

[45] https://commons.wikimedia.org/wiki/File:Pyrrhus.JPG

[46] *Photo zoomed in.* https://commons.wikimedia.org/wiki/File:Alma-tadema-antony-cleopatra.jpeg

[47] *Original: Andre Engels Vector: Wimmel, CC BY-SA 3.0 <http://creativecommons.org/licenses/by-sa/3.0/>, via Wikimedia Commons;* https://commons.wikimedia.org/wiki/File:Pythagorean_theorem_abc.svg

[48] *Source: user:shakko, CC BY-SA 3.0 <https://creativecommons.org/licenses/by-sa/3.0>, via Wikimedia Commons:* https://commons.wikimedia.org/wiki/File:Hippocrates_pushkin02.jpg

[49] *Photo zoomed in. Source: Steve Swayne, CC BY 2.0 <https://creativecommons.org/licenses/by/2.0>, via Wikimedia Common:* https://commons.wikimedia.org/wiki/File:The_Parthenon_in_Athens.jpg

[50] *Drummyfish, CC0, via Wikimedia Commons:* https://commons.wikimedia.org/wiki/File:Platonic_Solids_Transparent.svg

[51] *Photo zoomed in. Source: ZDF/Terra X/Gruppe 5/ Susanne Utzt, Cristina Trebbi/ Jens Boeck, Dieter Stürmer / Fabian Wienke / Sebastian Martinez/ xkopp, polloq, CC BY 4.0 <https://creativecommons.org/licenses/by/4.0>, via Wikimedia Commons:* https://commons.wikimedia.org/wiki/File:Archimedes%27-Lever.png

[52] https://commons.wikimedia.org/wiki/File:Pi_eq_C_over_d.svg

Made in United States
North Haven, CT
13 May 2025